CHRONOLOGY OF

IRISH

HISTORY

IRISH
HISTORY

Compiled by
David Pritchard

LAGAN BOOKS

Published 2001 by
Geddes & Grosset for Lagan Books

© 2001 Geddes & Grosset
David Dale House, New Lanark ML119DJ, Scotland

Cover image courtesy of DigitalVision

ISBN 1 85534 390 8

Printed and bound in Scotland

Chronology

c120
Ireland appears on Ptolemy's map of the known world. Seven rivers and five towns are marked.

c300
Irish pirates begin to raid Roman Britain.

c350
Ogham, the first written form of the Irish language, appears on gravestones and inscriptions in Ireland and western Britain.

c400
The Dál Riada of northeast Ulster plant their first settlements in western Scotland.

c425
Emain Macha (Navan Fort), ancient capital of Ulster, is destroyed by the Connachta.

431
Palladius is sent from Rome as 'Bishop to those in Ireland who believe in Christ.'.
Starting date for *The Annals of Ulster* (written later).

432
St Patrick arrives in Ireland.

433
St Patrick lights the Paschal Fire on Slane Hill (tradition).

441
St Patrick spends Lent on the summit of Croagh Patrick (tradition).

447
St Patrick makes Armagh the ecclesiastical capital of Ireland.

c450
Niall 'of the Nine Hostages', founder of the Uí Néill dynasty, dies.

467
St Benew of Kilbennan, disciple of St Patrick, dies.

470
Tara is established as the capital of the Uí Néill dynasty.

c484
Enda founds a monastery on the Aran Islands, according to tradition the first monastery in Ireland.

493
The death of St Patrick (tradition; some sources give 461).

500
The beginning of the 'Golden Age' of the Irish Church. Over the next century, monasteries are established throughout Ireland.
Written Irish develops an alphabet based on Latin letters (Archaic Old Irish period).

521
The birth of St Colmcille at Gartan, Co. Donegal.
Buite, Abbot of Monasterboice Monastery, dies.

524
The death of St Brigid of Kildare (traditional date).

527
Emly Monastery, Co. Tipperary, founded by this date.

530
The death of Enda of Aran.

537
Eogan, King of Connaught, is killed by his rival, Guaire, near Sligo.

540
Dermot of Inchleraun founds a monastery on Lough Ree, Longford.

543

St Columbanus is born in Leinster.

545

Glasnevin Monastery, Co. Dublin, is struck by an epidemic of the
plague which kills its abbot, Berchan.

546

St Colmcille founds the Monastery of Daire Calgach on the site of
modern Derry.

547

St Cíaran founds Monastery of Clonmacnoise on the River
Shannon.

548

The plague epidemic claims many lives. It continues until the end of
the next year.

549

Abbots Tighernach of Clones Monastery, Cíaran of Clonmacnoise
Monastery and Colum of Terryglass Monastery die, possibly from
the effects of the plague epidemic.

551

Nessan the Leper founds Bangor Monastery.

559

St Brendan founds the Monastery of Clonfert.

c560

The Vulgate Bible of St Jerome reaches Ireland from Italy.
Latin becomes established as the language of the Irish Church.

561

St Colmcille is censured at the Synod of Tailtíu.

563

St Colmcille sails to Scotland and establishes a monastery on the
island of Iona.

575

Assembly of Druim Cett. The King of the Uí Néill claims sovereignty over the Dál Riada. St Colmcille prevents a plan to expel the poets of Ireland.

577

The death of St Brendan of Clonfert, also known as 'the Voyager'.

587

St Columbanus leaves Ireland on a missionary journey to the continent of Europe.

c590

St Colmcille writes the *Cathach*, the earliest Irish manuscript of any importance.

591

St Columbanus establishes a monastery at Luxeuil in Gaul.

597

The death of St Colmcille on Iona.

c600

'Insular Latin' emerges as the language of the Irish Church.
The monk, Asprorius, writes the first Latin grammar in Ireland.
The death of Canice of Aghaboe, founder of Kilkenny.

610

St Columbanus travels to northern Italy and founds the Monastery of Bobbio.

615

St Columbanus dies in Bobbio, Italy.

c618

The death of Kevin, founder of Glendalough.

624

The birth of Eunan of Raphoe, author of *Vita Sancti Columbae* (Life of St Columba).

626

The death of Aedán of Ferns.

630

The Synod of Magh Léna is held to settle the date of Easter.

635

St Aidan begins a mission to convert the Northumbrians. He founds
the Monastery of Lindisfarne.

636

St Carthage founds the Monastery of Lismore.

637

Congalo Claen, King of the Dál Riada of Antrim, is killed at the Battle
of Mag Roth.
The Uí Néill gain dominance in Ulster.

649

The death of Ragallach Mac Uatach, the first documented king of the
Uí Briúin dynasty of Connaught.

c650

The treatise *Hisperica Famina*, an eccentric Latin grammar, is written
in Ireland.
The death, in France, of the missionary monk, St Fursu. He was buried
in the Irish Monastery at Péronne.

658

The death of Dimma, Bishop of Connor, Co. Antrim.

663

Thousands are killed by a new outbreak of the plague. It lasts for
several years.

664

In England, the Synod of Whitby rules against Irish monastic
practices.
Colman, Irish Abbot of Lindisfarne, resigns his office. He returns to
Ireland with his followers and founds a monastery on Inisboffin.

Bede's *Chronicle* comments that many English have gone to Ireland
   for religious study. He praises the generosity of the Irish people.

667
The plague outbreak ends after causing widespread devastation.

c670
The first mention of St Patrick's Day (17 March), in *The Life of St
   Gertrude of Nivelles.*

c675
The Book of Durrow is illuminated (now in Trinity College, Dublin).

679
Eunan of Raphoe is appointed Abbot of Iona.

c680
Antiphonary of Bangor written.
Scholars compile the Brehon Law Code, Leth Moga.

689
St Kilian, a missionary abbot, is martyred at Würzburg, Germany.

c690
Muirchú writes his *Life of St Patrick*, the basis of all later accounts.
   He describes the saint as 'Bishop of all Ireland'.

697
The Synod of Birr is convened.
Adomnán's Law, also known as 'the Law of the Innocent', places
   women, children and clergy under protection in time of war.

c700
The beginning of the Classical Old Irish linguistic period.
The Moylough Belt Shrine is made by Irish craftsmen.

714
The Kilnassaggart Pillar Stone is carved in Co. Armagh. It is the
   oldest dated monument in Ireland.

716

The monks of Iona accept the Roman Church date for Easter.

c720

The *Collectio Hibernensis* – a compilation of Irish Canon Law – is written on Iona.

c725

Irish craftsmen make the Ardagh Chalice.

c730

The *Senchas Mor* (great old knowledge) – a compilation of Brehon laws – is written.

740

The ascetic Culdee ('Servants of God') Movement develops in Munster in response to the increasing secularisation of Irish monasteries.

747

The death of Ferdáchrich of Dairinis, who was the teacher of the Culdee reformer, Máelrúain.

753

The death of Mac Oige of Lismore, one of the first Culdee abbots.

c755

The stone high crosses at Ahenny in Co. Tipperary, are sculpted in a style inspired by earlier wood and metal crosses.

760

The Clonmacnoise and Birr Monasteries go to war.

763

The first record is made of the Culdee monastery at Finglas, one of 'the two eyes of Ireland'.

764

Durrow Monastery suffers 200 dead when it fights a pitched battle with the monks of Clonmacnoise.

c770

Monks at Bangor, probably inspired by the works of the Greek
chronicler, Eusebio, compile an *Irish World Chronicle*.

774

The King of Leinster grants Máelrúain land to build Tallaght
Monastery, second of 'the two eyes of Ireland'.

780

Dublittir of Finlas presides over the Assembly of Tara.

792

The death of the Church reformer, Máelrúain of Tallaght.

795

The first Viking raid in Ireland is made on the monastery at Lambay
Island, Co. Dublin.

796

Death of Dublittir of Finglas, one of the leaders of the Culdee Reform
Movement .

c800

The Book of MacRegal of Birr is illuminated (now in Bodleian
Library, Oxford).
A high cross is raised at Moone, Co. Kildare. It is one of the earliest
high crosses to portray scenes from the scriptures.

802

Vikings attack and plunder Iona.

c805

The Book of Kells is illuminated by this date, probably in Iona.

807

Monks fleeing from Iona found the Monastery of Kells, Co. Meath.
Heláir of Loch Cré, a Culdee abbot, dies.

816

Vikings plunder the monastery on Scattery Island, Co. Clare.

820

Feidlimid Mac Crimthain becomes King of Munster.

823

Bangor is raided by Vikings and many monks are killed.

c825

The Irish scholar, Dicuil, writes a world geography for the King of the
Franks.

830

At least 26 monasteries have been plundered by Vikings since 795.

834

Clonmacnoise is plundered by Vikings.

837

A fleet of 65 Viking ships from Orkney and Norway lands in Dublin Bay.

840

The Viking army winters in Ireland for the first time, initiating a
transition from raiding to attempts at colonisation.

Feidlim, King of Munster, advances as far as Tara and kidnaps
Gormflaith, wife of Niall, the reigning Uí Néill.

The death of Maeldíthruib, the last of the reforming abbots, marks the
declining influence of the Culdees.

841

The foundation of Dublin as a Viking settlement when a longphort is
situated on the River Liffey. Another longphort is established at
Annagassen, Co. Louth.

845

Turgesius the Viking desecrates Clomacnoise and places his wife on
the High Altar.

Johannes Scotus Erigena appointed to the Royal school at Laon.

846

Turgesius is captured and drowned by Máel Seachnaill, King of the Uí
Néill.

c850
A Viking cemetery is established at Islandbridge, Dublin.

851
Danes from Northern England, led by Ivan of York, attack Ireland.

853
Olaf of Norway lands with his army, and assumes control of the settlement at Dublin.

861
Aed Finnliath, King of Ailech, allies with the Vikings of Dublin against the High King.

King Cerbhall of Ossory defeats Viking raiders at Grangefertagh Monastery, Co. Kilkenny.

862
Aed Finnliath is inaugurated as High King at Tara.

863
Viking raiders plunder prehistoric Boyne Valley passage graves.

866
Aed Finnliath drives out Viking raiders from Donegal to Antrim.

Ivan returns to the Kingdom of York.

871
Ivan of York returns and establishes his claim to Dublin.

872
The death of Ivan of York, described by Irish annalists as 'King of the Norsemen of all of Ireland and Britain'.

876
Viking activity declines, and there is very little raiding or new settlement for 40 years.

877
Flan, High King of Ireland, is defeated by King Lorcan at Magh Adhair, the inauguration place of Thomond.

900

The peak of Viking power in Ireland has passed.

The beginning of the Early Middle Irish linguistic period.

Latin scholarship is in decline with the increasing secularisation of the
monastic system.

902

The Irish destroy the Viking colony of Dublin. Many of its inhabitants
move to the Kingdom of York.

908

Flan, King of Tara, defeats and kills Cormac, King of Cashel, at the
Battle of Ballaghmoon.

Cormac bequeaths three ounces of gold and a satin chasuble to the
Monastery of Mungret.

c910

The resumption of Viking raids and settlement.

911

Vikings establish a settlement at Drogheda.

914

Vikings found the city of Waterford.

916

The accession of High King Niall Glundub Mac Aeda, founder of the
O'Neill septs of Ulster.

917

The death of King Tathal Ua Muiredaig, ancestor of the O'Tooles of
Leinster.

919

Danish Vikings defeat the Leinster Irish and establish the town of
Dublin.

c920

The high cross of Muireadach, one of the finest in Ireland, is sculpted
at Monasterboice, Co. Louth.

922

The town of Limerick is established by Vikings.

925

Sitric, King of Dublin and York, converts to Christianity.

928

Vikings massacre a thousand Irish in the Dunmore Cave, Co. Kilkenny.

934

The Dál Cais dynasty begins to rise to power in what is now modern Co. Clare.

941

Muircheartach of the Leather Cloaks, King of Ailech, circuits Ireland on a great raiding expedition.

944

The reign of Olaf, chief founder of the Kingdom of Dublin, begins.

948

Vikings destroy the Monastery of Slane, Co. Meath

950

Dublin is developing as a trading city, noted for its trade in slaves and luxury goods.

951

Vikings plunder St Mullins Monastery, Co. Carlow.

967

The Viking city of Limerick is plundered by the Dal Cáis.

968

Domnhall, King of Tara, expels Vikings from Monasterboice.

969

Tuamgraney Church in Clare (thought to be the oldest Irish church still used today) is rebuilt.

972

Vikings occupy Scattery Island, Clare.

973

The death of Conchobar Mac Teig, ancestor of the O'Connors.

c975

The monastery at Metz is founded by Catroe of Armagh.

976

Brian Boru succeeds his murdered brother, Mahon, as King of Dál
  Cais.

978

Brian Boru claims the Kingship of Munster.

980

Malachy, King of Meath, defeats the Dublin Vikings at the Battle of
  Tara. He is inaugurated High King.

981

Malachy captures the town of Dublin.

986

Brian Boru captures Limerick.

989

Malachy captures Dublin again.

995

Malachy captures Dublin for a third time and amongst his plunder he
  seizes the 'Ring of Thor'.

997

Malachy and Brian Boru agree to divide Ireland between them.

999

Brian Boru defeats combined armies of Leinster and Dublin at
  Glenmama, Co. Wicklow.
The first Irish coins are minted in Dublin by King Sitric Silkenbeard.

1000

King Sitric Silkenbeard submits after Brian Boru conquers Dublin.
The city is now well established on the Viking trade routes. Icelandic
records praise the quality of goods on a vessel from Dublin.

1001

Brian Boru attacks the territory of the Uí Néill.

1002

Malachy concedes High Kingship to Brian Boru.

1003

Reginald the Dane builds a great tower in Waterford.

1005

Brian Boru gives 20 ounces of gold to the Church. He recognises the
Bishop of Armagh as Primate of all Ireland

1006

Brian Boru carries out a Royal circuit of Ulster unchallenged.

1007

The Book of Kells is stolen from Kells Monastery (but recovered two
months later).

1013

Gormflath, the estranged wife of Brian Boru, encourages her brother,
Maelmora, King of Leinster and Sitric, King of Dublin, into
rebellion against the High King.

1014

Brian Boru defeats the Vikings of Dublin and Orkney, along with the
Irish of Leinster, at the Battle of Clontarf. After the battle, he is slain
in his tent by a fleeing Norseman named Broder. His body is taken to
Armagh for burial.
Malachy resumes High Kingship.

1022

The death of Malachy. The authority of the High Kingship effectively
lapses.

1028
King Sitric Silkenbeard of Dublin makes the pilgrimage to Rome.

1029
Sitric Silkenbeard's son is kidnapped by the Irish. He is ransomed for silver, 2,000 cattle and 120 British horses.

c1030
Dúnán becomes the first Bishop of Dublin.

1037
The Church of the Holy Trinity (later Christchurch Cathedral) is founded in Dublin.

1046
The Synod of Sutri initiates the Gregorian reform of the Church.

1049
An Irish Monk, Aaron of Cologne, is consecrated Bishop of Cracow, Poland.

1050
The beginning of Late Middle Irish linguistic period.

1064
The death of Donnchada, son of Brian Boru and titular High King. Turlough O'Brien accedes as first of the 'kings with opposition'.

1068
The sons of Harold, the Saxon king of England, are slain by William the Conqueror, who attacks Bristol with a fleet supplied by the Vikings of Ireland.

1073
The last-known Abbot of Castledermot Monastery in Co. Kildare dies.

1074
The Bishopric of Dublin falls under the authority of Archbishop of Canterbury.

1075
The Irish cleric, Marianus Scottus II, is granted the Church of St Peter at Regensburg, Germany.

1076
Murrough MacFlann, claimant to the High Kingship, is murdered in the round tower of Kells Monastery.

c1080
The beginning of a flourishing period in ecclesiastical metalworking inspired by a mixture of Irish and Norse artistic styles.

1088
Ulstermen destroy Mungret Abbey, Limerick.

1092
Monks on Leane Island, Killarney, begin to compile *The Annals of Inisfallen*.

1095
The Church of St Michan (Dublin) is founded.

1096
Malchus is created Bishop of Waterford by the Archbishop of Canterbury.

1098
There are many casualties when Munstermen burn down the monastery at Lusk, Co. Dublin.

c1100
Craftsmen make the Shrine of St Patrick's Bell, one of the earliest Irish examples of the Viking-inspired Urnes style.

1101
The first Synod of Cashel.
The Rock of Cashel, capital of Munster, is granted to the Church by Murtough O'Brien.
The Grianan of Aileach, Co. Donegal – capital of the O'Neills – is torn down by the army of Munster.

1102

Murrough O'Brien marries one of his three daughters to Arnulf of
Montgomery, a powerful Norman lord who sends Gerald of Windsor
to Ireland as his envoy.
St Anselm of Canterbury urges the reform of the Irish Church.

c1105

The Book of the Dun Cow is compiled at Clonmacnoise by Maol
Mhuire. It includes *The Táin*, the earliest long literary text in Irish.

1111

The Synod of Rathbreasail is attended by 50 bishops, 300 priests and
3,000 clerics.
Ireland is divided into the religious provinces of Armagh and Cashel.

1120

Turlough O'Connor revives the Feast of Tara, emphasising his claim
to be High King.

c1123

The Cross of Cong is made for Turlough O'Connor, King of
Connacht.
St Malachy is appointed Abbot of Bangor.

1124

The round tower at Clonmacnoise Monastery is built.
St Malachy is made Bishop of Down and Connor.

c1130

The Book of Leinster is compiled from earlier sources. It includes a
diagram of the banqueting hall of Tara.

1132

St Malachy is consecrated Archbishop of Armagh.

1133

Cattle herds are decimated by a bovine epidemic lasting for two years.

1134

Dermot MacMurrough accedes as King of Leinster.

The Clonmacnoise round tower is struck by lightning and badly damaged.

1135

Cormac's Chapel is completed on the Rock of Cashel.

1137

Dermot MacMurrough joins Connor O'Brien, King of Desmond, in a siege of the Viking port of Waterford. In return, O'Brien accepts MacMurrough as his overlord.

St Malachy establishes the Augustinian Priory of Downpatrick.

1139

St Malachy, en route for Rome, leaves four monks to train at the Cistercian Abbey of Clairvaux.

1142

Mellifont Abbey – the first Cistercian monastery in Ireland – is founded.

1148

St Malachy dies whilst visiting Rome for a second time.

Dermot MacMurrough invites Cistercians from Mellifont to establish Baltinglass Abbey, Co. Wicklow.

1150

Bective Abbey, Meath, is founded by the Cistercians.

1151

The Battle of Móin Mor. Turlough O'Connor and Dermot MacMurrough defeat Turlough O'Brien, the King of Munster. Annalists claim that over 7,000 of the Munster army were killed.

1152

Dermot MacMurrough abducts Dervilla, wife of Tiernan O'Rourke, King of Bréifne.

Paparo, first papal legate sent to Ireland, presides over the Synod of Kells. He divides Ireland into the Archbishoprics of Armagh, Cashel, Dublin and Tuam.

Mellifont Abbey now has seven daughter houses in Ireland.

Owen, an English knight, gives the earliest documented personal account of a pilgrimage to Patrick's Purgatory.

1153
Dervilla is returned to her husband.

1155
Pope Adrian IV issues the Bull Laudabiliter, granting King Henry II permission to go to Ireland in order to reform the Church.

1156
Murtough MacLoughlin becomes High King but with opposition. His rivals are Rory O'Connor and Tiernan O'Rourke.
Kells Monastery is burnt by raiders.

1157
The Cistercian church at Mellifont is consecrated with great ceremony.

1158
Jerpoint Abbey is established for the Benedictine order by Donal MacGillapatrick.

1161
Cistercians from Mellifont establish Boyle Abbey in Co. Roscommon.

1162
The Synod of Clane reaffirms the Primacy of Armagh and rules that lectors in Irish churches must be trained in Armagh.

1163
Laurence O'Toole, Abbot of Glendalough, is appointed Archbishop of Dublin.

1166
Rory O'Connor becomes High King. He captures Dermot MacMurrough's castle at Ferns and drives him from the Kingdom of Leinster. MacMurrough flees to England seeking military help to regain his kingdom.

1167

Dermot MacMurrough enlists the help of the Anglo-Norman Lord
  Strongbow (Richard De Clare).

MacMurrough returns to Ireland with a small detachment of Flemish
  mercenaries and re-establishes himself in Ferns.

1169

Anglo-Norman forces invade Leinster at the urgent request of Dermot
  MacMurrough.

Some 400 men, under Robert Fitzstephen, land at Bannow Bay, Co.
  Wexford (May 1). Maurice Fitzgerald lands near Wexford town with
  about 140 men. Wexford is occupied by the Anglo-Norman forces.

The building of a cathedral on the Rock of Cashel is initiated.

1170

Richard de Clare lands near Waterford with 200 knights and 1,000
  foot soldiers (August 23).

The combined Anglo-Norman armies capture the fortified towns of
  Dublin and Waterford.

Sixty-three religious houses now observe the Augustinian rule, many
  of them reformed Irish monasteries.

1171

Richard de Clare marries Aoife, daughter of Dermot MacMurrough.

Dermot MacMurrough dies (May), leaving Richard de Clare as his heir.

High King Rory O'Connor and Haskulf, King of Dublin, lay siege to
  Dublin. The Anglo-Norman garrison of Dublin destroys O'Connor's
  camp at Castleknock and the Norse/Irish army is dispersed.

King Henry II of England lands at Crook, near Waterford, with a large
  army and establishes his headquarters in Dublin. The Kings of
  Leinster, Bréifne, Ulster and Airgialla submit to Henry II.

The second Synod of Cashel is held.

1172

Henry II establishes his overlordship of Ireland. Dublin is granted a
  Royal Charter.

Hugh de Lacy is granted the Kingdom of Meath – he builds a motte
  and bailey at Trim.

Pope Alexander III writes to the Irish kings, advising them to
  recognise Henry.

There are now 15 Cistercian daughter houses to Mellifont Abbey.

1173
Pope Alexander III writes praising Henry II on his conquest of
  Ireland.

1175
Rory O'Connor submits to Henry II in the Treaty of Windsor.

1176
The death of Richard de Clare, leaving his daughter Isabella, a minor,
  as heir. Meath passes into the hands of the Crown, to be
  administered until Isabella de Clare comes of age.

1177
Prince John appointed Lord of Ireland at the age of 10.
John de Courcy invades Ulster and builds a castle at Downpatrick.

1179
Balla Monastery, Mayo, is destroyed by fire.

c1180
John de Courcy starts construction of Carrickfergus Castle, Co. Antrim.
Cistercians from Baltinglass replace the Benedictines at Jerpoint
  Abbey. Cistercians from Monasternagh found the Holy Cross Abbey,
  Tipperary.
Cormac's *Missal* illuminated (now in the British Library, London).

1185
Prince John is sent to govern Ireland. He grants unconquered Irish
  lands to Norman lords and builds castles at Lismore and Ardfinnan.
John de Courcy asks Jocelin de Furness to write a life of St Patrick.

1186
The Irish assassinate Hugh de Lacy after he erects a castle on the site
  of Durrow Monastery.

1189
William Marshall receives Strongbow's Irish estates when he marries
  Isabella de Clare.

Donal Mór O'Brien builds Clare Abbey for the Augustinian canons.

1190
Malachy of Armagh is canonised.

c1191
Giraldus Cambresis writes the first version of his account of Ireland, *Expugnatio Hibernica*.

1192
Founding of St Patrick's Cathedral, Dublin.

1193
Augustinians from Bodmin, Cornwall, establish the Priory at Kells, Co. Kilkenny.

1197
Limerick is granted a Royal Charter from King John, affording it all the liberties of Dublin.
Rory O'Connor, the last High King of Ireland, dies and is buried at Clonmacnoise.

1199
Dublin is established as an administrative county.

1200
The Irish Exchequer is established.
William Marshall founds Tintern Abbey, Co. Wexford, with monks from the great Cistercian Monastery of Tintern in South Wales – in fulfillment of a vow made during a stormy crossing of the Irish Sea.
The Classical Modern Irish linguistic period begins around this time.

1202
King John's castle at Limerick is completed.

1203
Gerald Fitzgerald builds a castle at Maynooth, Co. Kildare – in later centuries the seat of the Earls of Kildare.

1204
Clonmacnoise is burnt down for the 26th time in its history.

1205
Hugh de Lacey is granted all the land of Ulster.
William Marshall founds the Cistercian monastery at Graiguenemagh.

1206
The See of Meath moved from Clonard to Newtown Trim.

1207
The counties of Cork and Waterford are established. Irish coinage is
   minted bearing the symbol of the harp.

1210
King John returns to Ireland and drives the De Laceys out of their
   lordships of Meath and Ulster.
John de Grey builds a bridge over the River Shannon at Athlone.
Theobold Walter begins building a round keep at Nenagh.

1211
The counties Tipperary and Limerick are established.

1212
An Anglo-Norman army allies itself to Scots invaders in a concerted
   attack on the Irish of Ulster.
The Archbishop of Dublin initiates the building of Dublin Castle.

1213
King John submits to Pope Innocent III and receives England and
   Ireland as a papal fief.

1214
Glendalough is joined to the See of Dublin.

1215
At this date, only a quarter of the Irish bishoprics are held by
   Englishmen.

A Royal Charter grants the citizens of Dublin possession of the Liffey
fisheries up to Islandbridge.

1217

William Marshall issues a charter to Callan, Co. Kilkenny. The Irish
Treasury is established.

1220

The multi-angular keep of Trim Castle is completed by William Peppard.

1224

The St Mary Magdalene Dominican Friary is founded at Drogheda by
Luke Netterville, Archbishop of Armagh.

1227

Richard de Burgo is granted the whole land of Connaught for an
annual fee of 500 marks.
Jerpoint Abbey affiliates itself to Fountains Abbey, Yorkshire.

1228

The Abbot of Mellifont resigns after a Papal examination of abuses in
the abbey.

1230

Thomas Fitzmaurice is granted estates in Co. Limerick – his castle at
Shanid later becomes the 'chief house' of the Fitzgeralds of Desmond.
Ireland's only Trinitarian monastery is founded in Adare, Co. Limerick.

1231

Richard de Burgo builds a castle at Galway.
The Franciscan Friars establish their first Irish religious house at Youghal.

1233

The counties of Louth and Kerry are established.

1234

Richard Marshall is murdered at a truce meeting on the Curragh,
allegedly at the request of King Henry III, after a quarrel.
The full military muster of the English colony invades Connacht.

1237

Walter de Burgh builds castles at Loughrea and other strategic points
   in Connacht.
The De Barrys establish Ballybeg Augustinian Friary, Co. Cork.

1240

The Cistercian Abbot of Knockmoy, Co. Galway, is censured for
   having his hair washed by a woman.

1250

The Anglo-Normans now dominate most of Munster and Leinster and
   have penetrated Connacht and the eastern parts of Ulster.
Robert de Muscegros erects a castle at Bunratty, Co. Clare.

1251

A mint is opened in Dublin.
Buttevant Franciscan Friary is founded and dedicated to St Thomas a
   Becket.

1257

The Anglo-Norman advance northwards from Sligo into Ulster is
   stopped by the O'Donnells at the Battle of Credan.

1258

The Princes of Thomond and Connacht acknowledge Brian O'Neill of
   Ulster as King of Ireland.

1260

The joint armies of Connacht and Ulster are defeated at Downpatrick
   and Brian O'Neill is killed in battle.

1261

The MacCarthys of Kerry defeat the Royal army at Callan, killing
   many of the leading settlers in Desmond.
Norman expansion into west Munster ends and does not resume.

1262

Irish chiefs ask King Haakon of Norway (who is wintering with his
   fleet in Scotland) to lead them against the Normans.

1263
Walter de Burgh is made Earl of Ulster.

1265
New Ross is walled.

1269
Robert de Ufford builds Roscommon Castle.

1270
The Irish check the expansion of the Anglo-Normans into Thomond
and Roscommon at the Battle of Ath in Chip.

1271
Walter de Burgh dies after a short illness.

1272
By now there are 38 Cistercian monasteries in Ireland.

1277
Stone Castle is erected at Bunratty by Thomas de Clare.

c1279
The Walls of Galway are completed at a cost of 46 pounds.

1280
The De Clares build Quin Castle, Co. Clare, as part of an expansion
into the O'Brien territory of Thomond.
St Canice's Cathedral, Kilkenny, is completed.

1286
Richard de Burgh succeeds to the Earldom of Ulster – he becomes
known as the 'Red Earl'.

1290
The first mention in Irish annals of *gallowglass* or 'foreign soldiers',
mercenary axemen hired from the Scottish Highlands and Islands.

1292
County Roscommon is established.

1297

A Parliament is held in Dublin – representatives come from the
  liberties and counties.

1300

Ballymote Castle, Co. Sligo is built by Richard de Burgh.
The Dominicans have by now established 25 friaries in Ireland.
Towns are represented in Parliament for the first time.

1301

An Anglo-Norman contingent is sent from Dublin to aid Edward I in
  his war against Scotland.

1302

Elizabeth de Burgh, daughter of the Red Earl, marries Robert Bruce.

1305

Richard de Burgh builds Northburgh Castle (Greencastle) at the mouth
  of Lough Foyle, Co. Donegal.

1306

County Carlow is established.

1308

The O'Kellys destroy the town of Roscommon and capture its castle.
John le Decer, Mayor of Dublin, has the aqueduct supplying the city's
  drinking water repaired.

1310

A Parliament is held at Kilkenny. The Government legislates that the
  heads of Irish clans should be held responsible for the actions of
  their dependants.
Felim O'Connor is inaugurated as 'King' of Connaught.
Native Irishmen are barred from joining Anglo-Norman religious
  houses.

1315

Edward Bruce claims the crown of Ireland. He lands at Larne with a
  large Scottish army, attacks the Anglo-Norman colony and causes
  widespread devastation.

1316

Edward Bruce is crowned King of Ireland at Faughart.

St Patrick's Cathedral, Dublin, is badly damaged in a fire.

1317

Edward Bruce is joined by his brother Robert, King of Scotland.

Anglo-Norman castles and towns in the counties of Limerick and
Tipperary are destroyed by the Scottish army.

Donal O'Neill of Ulster writes to Pope John XXII requesting him to
recognise Edward Bruce as King of Ireland (the Irish
Remonstrance).

A general pardon, granted to rebels in Co. Cork, indicates that many
members of the Anglo-Norman Condon and Roche families have
already been Gaelicised.

1318

The Scots invasion and bad harvests, cause famine in the country.

Edward Bruce is killed in a battle at Faughart by John de Bermingham.

The O'Briens defeat the De Clares at the Battle of Dysert O'Dea.

Anglo-Normans abandon Bunratty and other Thomond castles north of
the River Shannon.

1320

Parliament is held in Dublin. The Archbishop of Dublin opens a short-
lived university in the city, with four masters.

The Church of St Nicholas of Myra is built in Galway about this time.

1323

Dame Alice Kyteler is convicted of witchcraft in Kilkenny – she
escapes but her maid, Petronella, is executed.

The Book of Kildare is compiled about this time.

1326

The Red Earl of Ulster dies, leaving a young heir.

1327

Robert the Bruce invades Ulster for a second time but he returns to
Scotland by winter. In the aftermath of the wars, Connacht has
passed out of English control.

1329

Maurice Fitz-Thomas is created First Earl of Desmond and granted the
  county of Kerry.

The Anglo-Norman Earl of Louth takes Irish harpers and poets into his
  service.

1330

A new belfry tower is erected at Christchurch Cathedral in
  Dublin.

1332

Walter Burke is starved to death in Northburgh Castle by order of the
  Brown Earl of Ulster.

1333

The Brown Earl is murdered in retaliation for Walter Burke at Le Ford
  (modern Belfast).

Norman possessions in Ulster beyond the River Bann are lost to the
  Irish.

1334

The Aran Islands are raided by Sir John Darcy, Lord Justiciar of
  Ireland.

1335

A force of 1,500 men are sent from Ireland to aid Edward III in his
  Scottish war.

1336

There are concerted attacks on Anglo-Norman settlements in
  Leinster.

1339

The Dublin Annals state there is 'general war throughout all
  Ireland'.

c1340

Eamonn and William de Burgo establish territories in Mayo and
  Galway.

1341

The Irish Parliament criticises the English administrators for their
mismanagement of Ireland.

1346

Relics of St Canice are lost after his church at Aghaboe is destroyed.

1347

The Government decrees that English settlers may not marry anyone
Irish without its express permission.

1348

The Black Death arrives in Ireland, with many deaths in Dublin.
The Fitzgeralds of Desmond acquire Askeaton Castle, Co. Limerick.
Edward III seizes Dunbrody Abbey because its monks refuse to give
alms to the poor or receive guests.

1349

The plague spreads throughout Anglo-Norman areas. The Bishop of
Armagh estimates that two-thirds of the English colony have been
killed by the Black Death. Eight friars die in one day in the
Dominican church in Kilkenny.

1350

The Black Death sweeps through Irish-held areas.
John O'Byrne, new Lord of the O'Byrnes of Wicklow, is paid to keep
his subjects at peace for two years.
Sir Thomas Rokeby is appointed Justiciar and ordered 'to establish the
peace of the land'.

1351

Rokeby instructs English settlers to avoid contact with the Irish.

Brehon law is banned in areas under Royal control.
William de Burgo founds the Ross Errily Franciscan Friar in Co. Galway.

1352

Rokeby defeats the MacCarthies of Cork and Kerry and pacifies
Munster.

1353

The O'Kellys found a Franciscan friary at Kilconnell, Co. Galway.

1354

A Royal army is defeated by the O'Byrnes in the Wicklow Mountains.

1355

The death of the First Earl of Desmond.

1357

Thomas Rokeby dies four days after concluding a campaign against
   the Irish of Leinster.

1358

Art MacMurrough raises war in Leinster and threatens Dublin.
Gerald Fitzgerald succeeds as the Third Earl of Desmond. A renowned
   poet, he introduces the love lyric to Gaelic literature.

1360

English colonists petition King Edward III for help against the Irish.
The death of Richard Ledrede, Bishop of Ossory, who tried to ban
   secular songs in Ireland.

1361

Lionel of Clarence (the 3rd son of Edward III) is appointed Justiciar.
The seat of Government is transferred to Carlow.
There is a second outbreak of the Black Death.

1366

The Irish Parliament passes the Statutes of Kilkenny, banning the use of
   Irish language, customs and dress by English and loyal Irish subjects.

1367

Administrative documents in Dublin begin to refer to 'Irish enemies'
   and 'English rebels'.

1370

The O'Briens and MacNamaras burn down Limerick and capture the
   castle.

1375

The important trading centre of Kilmallock in Co. Limerick is walled.

At this date, the Franciscan friary at Ennis, Co. Clare, has 350 friars and 600 pupils in its renowned school.

1379

Edward Mortimer, Earl of March, is appointed the King's Lieutenant in Ireland (he dies in 1381).

1392

Richard II appoints the Duke of Gloucester as his Lieutenant.

1394

Richard II arrives in Ireland.

1395

Art MacMurrough and other Leinster chieftains submit to Richard II near Carlow (February).

1398

The death of Gerald 'the Poet', Third Earl of Desmond.

Roger Mortimer is slain by the O'Byrnes.

1399

The second visit of Richard II to Ireland. He leaves Prince Hal (afterwards Henry V) and Humphrey, Duke of Gloucester, in Trim Castle for safekeeping.

1400

The *eric* (fine) for killing a 'man of learning' in Connacht is fixed at 126 cows.

The O'Neill Harp (now in Trinity College, Dublin) is made about now.

1402

The Dublin militia, under their mayor, kill 500 O'Byrnes in a battle at Bray, Co. Wicklow.

1405

First documented reference to Irish whiskey.

1411

Laurent de Pasztho, a Hungarian knight, gives one of the most
detailed medieval accounts of the pilgrimage to Patrick's
Purgatory.

1414

The bard Niall O'Higgins is alleged to have killed Sir John Stanley by
means of a malediction.

1416

The Great Book of Lecan compiled.

1418

The death of Art MacMurrough, chief opponent of the English colony
in Leinster.

1423

The death of Turlough O'Donnell, Lord of Tyrconnell, noted for
fathering 18 sons by 10 different women and having 59 grandsons.
The first Irish house of the reforming Augustinian Observant
Movement is established at Banada, Co. Sligo.

1425

Dominican Observants found a house at Portumna, Co. Galway.

1429

Building grant of ten pounds offered to landowners who will build
defensive towers in the area that is to become known as the Pale.

1430

This year sees the beginnings of a revival in monasticism.
Irish and Gaelicised lords establish Franciscan, Dominican and
Augustinian friaries throughout Ireland during the next 80 years.

1431

Foundation of the Choir of St Patrick's Cathedral.

1433

Franciscan Observants are established at Quin, Co. Clare, in a friary
built on the ruins of an abandoned De Clare castle.

1435

Landowners in the part of Ireland under English control are forbidden to employ Irish bards and rhymers.

1440

Tower-houses are built in large numbers from about this date.

1443

A great festival of Gaelic poets and musicians is held at Killeigh and over 2,700 attend.

1445

A native-born prelate is appointed as the head of the Irish Franciscans for the first time.

1446

The word 'Pale' is first used to denote the counties around Dublin still under the control of the Dublin administration.

Cormac Laidir MacCarthy builds Blarney Castle, Co. Cork.

1448

Muckross Franciscan Friary, Co. Kerry, is founded by the MacCarthies.

1449

Richard of York is appointed Lord Lieutenant of Ireland – he stays only a short time before returning to England to fight in the Wars of the Roses.

1452

The White Earl of Ormond dies at Ardee Castle.

1459

The Duke of York takes refuge in Ireland after the Lancastrians are victorious at the Battle of Ludlow.

1460

The Irish Parliament held at Drogheda declares its right to be the sole legislator for Ireland.

Yorkist and Lancastrian factions in Ireland are led by the
   Fitzgeralds of Desmond and Kildare and the Butlers of Ormond
   respectively.
Moyne Franciscan Friary is founded by the MacWilliam Burkes of
   Mayo.

1461
Edward IV of York defeats Lancastrians at Towton in England.

1462
Thomas, son of the Seventh Earl of Desmond, defeats the Earl of
   Ormond's army at the Battle of Pilltown – establishing the
   supremacy of the Fitzgeralds in Ireland.

1463
Thomas Fitzgerald succeeds to the Earldom of Desmond on his
   father's death – he is appointed Lord Lieutenant of Ireland by
   Edward IV.

1465
About this time, silver groats are minted in Waterford.
The MacCarthys found Kilcrea Franciscan Friary, Co. Cork.

1466
The defences of Meath are permanently weakened when the
   O'Connors of Offaly defeat the Earl of Desmond.
The Franciscan friary at Adare, Co. Limerick, is completed.

1467
John Tiptoft, Earl of Worcester, is sent to govern Ireland by Edward
   IV.
Thomas, the Eighth Earl of Desmond, is seized and summarily
   executed whilst attending Parliament at Drogheda.
Bunratty Castle, Co. Clare, is completed by Seán Finn
   MacNamara.

1474
The Guild of St George – a small standing army of 120 archers and 80
   men at arms – is established in the Pale.

1476

Brehon law has totally replaced common law in County Waterford.

1478

Garret Fitzgerald succeeds as Eighth Earl of Kildare – he dominates
  Ireland for the next 30 years and becomes known as the 'Great
  Earl'.

1484

St Nicholas Church, Galway, acquires collegiate status.

1485

Richard III defeated at the Battle of Bosworth Field in England.
Henry VII founds the Tudor dynasty.

1487

Lambert Simnel, pretender to the English throne, is crowned Edward
  VI at Christchurch Cathedral, Dublin.
Waterford, the second city in Ireland, asserts its loyalty to Henry
  VII.
Lambert Simnel invades England with an army including Irish Yorkists
  and German mercenaries and is defeated at the Battle of Stoke.
First recorded use of firearms in Ireland, when a soldier is shot dead at
  a siege in Donegal.

1491

Perkin Warbeck arrives in Cork, claiming to be Richard of York,
  younger of the two sons of Edward IV. He is accepted by the Earl of
  Desmond and other Munster lords.

1493

The Mayor of Galway hangs Walter Lynch, his own son, for murder.

1494

Sir Edward Poynings is appointed Lord Deputy with orders to reassert
  Royal authority in Ireland. He calls a Parliament in Drogheda.
Poynings' Law is passed, asserting that no Parliament may be called in
  Ireland without the express permission of the King and his Council
  in England. This marks the end of the Middle Ages in Ireland and
  the beginning of the Modern Era.

1495

Waterford is unsuccessfully besieged by followers of Perkin Warbeck.
It is decreed that the Constable of the strategic Carlingford Castle, Co.
  Louth, must be an Englishman.

1496

Henry VII re-appoints the Great Earl to Lord Deputy, saying 'Since all
  Ireland cannot rule this man, this man must rule Ireland.'

1500

A fire in Galway destroys large parts of the city's residential area. *The
  Book of Lismore* is written around this date.

1501

The O'Connors capture Sligo Castle in a surprise attack.

1502

Bad weather causes famine and disease in many areas.

1503

Garret Og Fitzgerald, heir to the Great Earl of Kildare, returns home
  from England, where he has been in custody.

1504

The Battle of Knockdoe. The Great Earl's army defeats an alliance led
  by his son-in-law, Ulrick Burke of Clanrickard. The Great Earl
  receives the Order of the Garter from Henry VII.

1505

Red Hugh O'Donnell, King of Tyrconnell, dies after a reign of 44
  years.

1507

Thomas O'Farrell begins building the last medieval Dominican friary
  in Ireland at Ballindoon, Co. Sligo.

1508

The O'Donnells capture Enniskillen Castle from the Maguires.
The last medieval Franciscan friary in Ireland is founded at Creevelea,
  Co. Leitrim, by Owen O'Rourke.

1510

The Earl of Kildare leads a campaign against Irish rebels in Munster.
He recaptures several castles but is defeated by the O'Briens of
Clare near Limerick .

1511

Hugh Dubh O'Donnell, the Great Earl's principle ally in Ulster, is
knighted by Henry VIII.

1512

O'Donnell raises a mercenary army. He defeats the Burkes of
Connacht and then forces the submission of Art O'Neill of
Tyrone.

1513

The death from gunshot wounds of Garret, the Great Earl of Kildare,
the 'best and foremost of all the Galls that had ever arisen for power,
renown and dignity' (*The Annals of Connacht*).

1514

At this time, there are reported to be 60 Irish and 30 English
descended 'chief captains' ruling over independent lordships outside
of Royal authority.

1515

James and John Fitzgerald, rival sons of the Earl of Desmond,
fight for the control of the Geraldine fortress at Lough Gur
(Limerick).

1516

Piers Butler is appointed the Eighth Earl of Ormond.

1517

Dundrum Castle, Co. Down, is recaptured from the Irish
MacGuinness sept.

1519

Garret, Earl of Kildare and Lord Deputy since 1513, is ordered to
England on charges of malfeasance.

1520

The Earl of Surrey, Henry VIII's new Lord Lieutenant, arrives in
  Dublin.

He brings with him orders to subdue Ireland by persuasion rather than
  violence.

The Corporation of Galway bans Brehon jurists from representing
  clients in its law courts.

1521

The Earl of Surrey ravages the territories of the O'Connors, the
  O'Mores and the O'Carrolls.

The German artist, Albrecht Durer, sketches a pair of Irish
  mercenaries.

1522

English warships are sent to prevent mercenaries crossing over from
  Scotland to Ireland.

The Earl of Ormond is appointed Lord Deputy.

1523

The Earl of Kildare returns home after four years' detention in
  England.

1524

The Earls of Ormond and Kildare make peace – Ormond marries
  Kildare's sister.

1525

The Archdeacon of the Diocese of Leighlin assassinates his Bishop; he
  is later executed along with his accomplices.

1526

Garret Og, Earl of Kildare, is committed to the Tower of London on
  suspicion of treason.

Rory O'Tunney carves the tomb of Piers Fitz-Oge Butler at Kilcooly
  Abbey, Tipperary.

1527

Garret Og is cleared of all charges and released.

1528

A long-standing dispute between the English and Irish branches of the
  Butler family is finally resolved when Thomas Boleyn accedes as
  the Earl of Ormond.
A gale hits the west of Ireland on the Friday before Christmas, sinking
  many ships and destroying the chapter house of Donegal Abbey.

1529

James, Earl of Desmond, receives Gonzalo Fernandez, the chaplain of
  Emperor Charles V.

1530

William Skeffington is appointed Lord Deputy.
The death of George Brann, the miserly 'Greek' Bishop of Elphin. He
  is called 'a stumbling block to humanity' in *The Annals of
  Connacht*.

1531

Skeffington campaigns in Tyrone and Donegal.

1532

English forces demolish Dungannon Castle, the main seat of O'Neill
  of Tyrone.

1533

The Irish Parliament confirms the supremacy of the See of Armagh
  over Dublin.

1534

The Ninth Earl of Kildare is arrested for treason and dies in Tower of
  London (September).
'Silken Thomas' Fitzgerald rebels against Henry VIII and attacks
  Dublin Castle.

1535

William Skeffington captures Maynooth Castle, chief seat of the
  Fitzgeralds of Kildare, and massacres its garrison.
Silken Thomas Fitzgerald's rebellion is crushed by Lord Grey's
  army.

1536

The estates of the Earldom of Kildare are confiscated. Lord Grey is
  appointed Lord Deputy.
The 'Reformation Parliament' takes place in Dublin.
Several large Irish monasteries are ordered to be suppressed and their
  properties confiscated.
George Brown is appointed as the first Protestant Bishop of
  Dublin.

1537

Silken Thomas Fitzgerald and five of his uncles are executed at
  Tyburn, London.

1538

The O'Connors of Offaly submit to Lord Deputy Grey.
The dissolution of All Hallows Priory, Dublin (site of the future
  Trinity College).
St Patrick's Staff and other Irish relics are publicly burnt in Dublin.

1539

Lord Deputy Grey defeats the combined forces of the O'Neills and
  O'Donnells at Bellahoe on the borders of the Pale.
The Irish Government is ordered to suppress all religious houses.
  Gracedieu, one of the few Benedictine convents in Ireland, is closed
  along with its famous girls' school.

1540

Henry VIII inaugurates a 'surrender and regrant' policy, offering titles
  and favourable terms to Irish and Gaelicised English lords who
  submit to English authority and law.

1541

The Irish Parliament changes Henry VIII's title 'Lord of Ireland' to
  'King of Ireland'.

1542

Many important Irish and Anglo-Norman chieftains submit.
Con O'Neill created Earl of Tyrone.
The first Jesuits arrive in Ireland.

1543

The Earldom of Thomond (O'Brien of Clare) and the Earldom of
Clanricard (Burke of Galway) are created under the surrender and
regrant policy.

1544

Following the death of the First Earl of Clanricard, a war breaks out
amongst his heirs.

1546

Thomas Butler (Black Tom), cousin of the future Queen Elizabeth I,
becomes the Tenth Earl of Ormond.

1547

Henry VIII dies. The accession of Edward VI. The beginning of the
'Edwardian Reformation'.

1548

Lord Deputy St Leger recalled on suspicion of treason.

1549

The First Act of Uniformity imposes *The Book of Common Prayer*.

1550

St Leger is reinstated as Lord Deputy.
The plantation (establishing of settlements) of Leix and Offaly begins
(ends 1557).

1551

The Scots carry out a massacre on Tory Island (Donegal).
The Book of Common Prayer is the first book to be printed in Ireland.
English liturgy is introduced into Irish churches.

1552

The Cathedral at Clonmacnoise is looted and desecrated by Protestant
Reformers.

1553

Mary Tudor succeeds to the English throne and begins restoring the
Catholic religion in Ireland (the 'Marian Restoration').

1554

The Fitzgeralds are reinstated to the Earldom of Kildare.

Married clergy are banned and ordered to be removed from office.

1555

A Papal Bull reconciles Ireland with Rome.

1556

Shane O'Neill, son of Con Bacach, is forced to submit by Lord Deputy Radcliffe.

1557

Armagh is burnt by the English.

Shane O'Neill attacks the O'Donnells of Donegal.

Lord Deputy Sussex begins the plantation of Offaly.

1558

Queen Elizabeth I succeeds to the English throne.

Sir Henry Sidney is appointed Lord Justiciar of Ireland.

Shane O'Neill murders Matthew, Baron of Dungannon – his half-brother and rival to the Earldom of Tyrone.

1559

Shane O'Neill seizes the chieftainship of the O'Neills on the death of his father Con Bacach.

Hugh O'Neill, the son of Baron Dungannon, is taken to England for his safety and raised as an English nobleman.

1560

The Acts of Uniformity and Supremacy restore the Protestant faith in Ireland and they enforce the use of *The Book of Common Prayer*.

1561

Shane O'Neill is declared a traitor.

1562

Shane O'Neill goes to London, where his Irish bodyguards cause much comment at Court and he submits to Elizabeth I.

1563

Shane O'Neill is defeated at Tullahogue by Sussex.

Adam Loftus appointed Archbishop of Armagh.

1564

The Irish of Leix and Offaly rebel against the plantation of their territories.

Shane O'Neill campaigns against the MacDonnells of Antrim.

1565

Thomas Earl of Ormond defeats his rival Gerald, Earl of Desmond, at the Battle of Affane.

Shane O'Neill crushes the Scots of Antrim, at Glenshesk, near Ballycastle.

1566

Richard Creagh, the Roman Catholic nominee for Archbishop of Armagh, escapes from the Tower of London.

Shane O'Neill burns Armagh Cathedral and attacks the English garrison at Derry.

1567

Gerald, Fourteenth Earl of Desmond, is arrested on suspicion of treason and sent to the Tower of London.

The O'Donnells defeat Shane O'Neill at Farsetmore. He flees to the MacDonnells and is killed by them at Cushendun, Antrim.

Archbishop Loftus is moved from Armagh to Dublin.

1568

James Fitzmaurice begins a rebellion to restore the Earl of Desmond.

Thomas, Earl of Ormond, builds an Elizabethan mansion at Carrick on Suir, Co. Tipperary.

Sir Peter Carew is granted the Barony of Idrone in Co. Carlow.

1569

Sir Henry Fitton is appointed President of Connacht, which is shired by a Royal Commission.

Sir Peter Carew plans to colonise the surrendered estates of the Earl of Desmond.

1570

The Fitzgeralds attack and plunder the town of Kilmallock in
   Limerick.
Elizabeth I excommunicated by Pope Pius V.

1571

Sir John Perrot, reputedly the illegitimate son of Henry VIII, is
   appointed President of Munster.
Elizabeth I authorises a scheme to colonise the Ards Peninsula in
   eastern Ulster.
In Dublin, a Gaelic language book is printed for the first time in
   Ireland.
Catholic Bishop Miler Magrath changes faith and is appointed
   Protestant Archbishop of Cashel.

1572

Sir John Perrot campaigns against the Munster rebels and captures
   Castlemaine.

1573

The first Desmond rebellion ends.
James Fitzmaurice surrenders to Perrot.
Gerald, Earl of Desmond, returns to Ireland. He is arrested but escapes
   to his castle at Tralee.
The Earl of Essex lands at Carrickfergus with plans to colonise
   Ulster.

1574

The Earl of Essex treacherously kills several hundred Irishmen at a
   banquet he holds in Belfast.

1575

James Fitzmaurice travels to Europe seeking help for a Catholic
   rebellion.
Essex is ordered to abandon his attempts to establish settlements in
   Ulster.
Sir James Norrys massacres the MacDonnell inhabitants of Rathlin
   Island.

1576

Nicholas Maltby is appointed Governor of Connaught.

Protestant refugees from the Low Countries arrive in Dublin.

Grace O'Malley, the notorius 'pirate queen' of Mayo, visits the court
of Elizabeth I.

1577

The Papacy pledges its support to James Fitzmaurice.

Holinshead's Chronicles are published, containing information on
Ireland by Richard Stanihurst.

1578

A Papal force leaves Italy en route to Ireland.

1579

A contingent of Papal soldiers lands at Smerwick, Kerry, under the
leadership of James Fitzmaurice.

Rebellion breaks out in Munster after the Fitzgeralds kill two English
envoys in Tralee, Kerry.

James Fitzmaurice is killed in a skirmish at Barrington's Bridge near
Limerick.

The Earl of Desmond assumes leadership of the rebels.

Sir Nicholas Maltby defeats the Fitzgeralds at Monasternenagh.

The Earl of Desmond sacks Youghal, Cork.

1580

The Earl of Ormond institutes a scorched earth policy in Munster.

Some 600 Papal troops land at Smerwick and establish themselves at
Dún an ir (September).

James Eustace, Viscount Baltinglass and the O'Byrnes revolt in
Leinster.

Lord Deputy Grey is defeated in Glenmalure, Wicklow, by the
O'Byrnes.

The Papal force at Smerwick surrenders and is massacred by English
forces led by Grey and Sir Walter Raleigh.

1581

English forces gain the upper hand in Munster and the leaders of the
rebellion become fugitives.

Nicholas Sanders, the Papal Legate, dies in Co. Limerick.

John Derricke publishes *The Image of Irelande*, an illustrated account (in verse) of a military campaign in Ireland.

1582

John of Desmond, brother to the Earl of Desmond, is killed by English forces.

The scorched earth policy in Munster causes a famine that claims 30,000 lives in six months. There are reports of cannibalism.

1583

The Desmond rebellion ends.

Gerald, the Fourteenth Earl of Desmond, is murdered by the O'Moriartys near Tralee after his followers steal some cattle.

1584

Dermot O'Hurley, Archbishop of Cashel, is hanged in Dublin.

1585

The Composition of Connaught; the majority of Irish chieftains in the region agree to submit to English administration and practices.

The death of Richard Creagh, Roman Catholic Archbishop of Armagh, a prisoner in the Tower of London for 18 years.

Rathfarnham Castle, Co. Dublin, is built by Archbishop Loftus.

1586

Scottish mercenaries are massacred by Sir Richard Bingham, Lord President of Connaught, at Ardnaree, Mayo.

1587

The Munster plantation begins and undertakers include Sir Walter Raleigh and the poet Edmund Spenser.

Hugh O'Neill is granted the title of Earl of Tyrone.

1588

At least 23 ships of the fleeing Spanish Armada are wrecked off the western coasts of Ireland. (September).

The galleon *Girona* founders off Dunluce Castle, Co. Antrim.

Sir Walter Raleigh is made Mayor of Youghal, Co. Cork.

1589

The Burkes of Mayo and the O'Rourkes rebel, citing mistreatment by
  Richard Bingham as the cause.

c1590

Sir Walter Raleigh plants the first potatoes grown in Ireland (reputedly
  at Killua Castle, Co. Westmeath).
Edmund Spenser publishes Part 1 of *The Faerie Queen*.

1591

Red Hugh O'Donnell, heir to the Earl of Tyrconnell, escapes from
  Dublin Castle and finds refuge in the Wicklow Mountains with the
  O'Byrnes.

1592

Red Hugh O'Donnell succeeds to the chieftainship of the O'Donnells.
The Irish College at Salamanca, Spain, is founded.

1593

Hugh O'Neill is inaugurated as 'The O'Neill'. Red Hugh O'Donnell
  leads a rebellion of O'Donnells and Maguires in Ulster.
The Irish College at Lisbon, Portugal, is founded.

1594

Bingham's army routed by Hugh Maguire at the 'Ford of the Biscuits'.
Trinity College, Dublin, opens for enrolments.
The Irish College at Douai, Belgium, is founded.

1595

Hugh O'Neill openly joins the Ulster rebellion.
Sir Henry Bagenal's army defeated at Clontibret, Monaghan.
O'Neill and O'Donnell petition King Phillip II of Spain for aid.

1596

The Ulster leaders meet Alonso Cobos, Spanish envoy.
O'Neill calls on Munster lords to join his revolt.

1597

Fiach MacHugh O'Byrne ambushed and killed in Co. Wicklow.
Hugh O'Donnell repels an English army at Ballyshannon, Donegal.

Sir John Chichester, Governor of Carrickfergus, is killed by the
   MacDonnells of Antrim.

1598

The Battle of the Yellow Ford – the combined forces of O'Neill,
   O'Donnell and Maguire overwhelm an English army led by Sir
   Henry Bagenal outside of Armagh.
Rebellion breaks out throughout Ireland.

1599

Robert Dudley, Earl of Essex, is sent to restore order in Ireland.
   English forces defeated at the Pass of the Plumes and Deputy's Pass.
   The Earl of Essex agrees a truce with Hugh O'Neill and returns to
   England.
Sir Thomas Norrys builds a fortified mansion at Mallow, Co. Cork.

1600

Mountjoy is appointed Lord Deputy and given a large army to subdue
   the rebels.
Henry Dowcra lands in Lough Foyle and fortifies Derry. Mountjoy
   fights O'Neill at the Moyry Pass, enters Ulster and builds a fort at
   Mount Norris, Armagh.
Rebel forces in Munster and Wicklow are defeated and then
   dispersed.
James, Fifteenth Earl of Desmond, is repudiated by his subjects when
   he attends a Protestant church service in Kilmallock.

1601

A Spanish army under Don Juan del Aguila lands at Kinsale, Co. Cork
   (September). Lord Mountjoy lays siege to Kinsale.
Hugh O'Neill and Hugh O'Donnell bring their armies from Ulster to
   aid the Spanish. Dunboy Castle on Bere Island, Co. Cork, is
   occupied by a Spanish garrison.
At the Battle of Kinsale, Lord Mountjoy routes the armies of Ulster a
   few miles outside of the town (24 December).
Hugh O'Neill retires to Ulster, while Hugh O'Donnell takes ship
   for Spain.

1602

Del Aguila surrenders to Mountjoy at Kinsale.

Dunboy Castle is stormed and its defenders are put to the sword.

Hugh O'Donnell dies in Spain.

Lord Mountjoy invades Tyrone and destroys the stone inauguration seat of the O'Neills at Tullahogue.

Rory O'Donnell, brother and successor of Red Hugh, surrenders to Mountjoy.

Donal Cam O'Sullivan Beare begins his epic march from Glengarrif, in Cork to Ulster accompanied by about a thousand followers (December).

1603

O'Sullivan Beare arrives in Leitrim with 36 men (January).

The death of Elizabeth I. She is succeeded by King James I.

Hugh O'Neill submits to Lord Mountjoy at Mellifont, Co. Louth.

The end of the Ulster Rebellion, sometimes called the Nine Years War.

Hugh O'Neill and Rory O'Donnell are pardoned and allowed to retain their titles and estates.

1604

The death of Katherine Fitzgerald, the old Countess of Desmond'. She was reputedly 140 years old.

A Friday market is opened in Belfast.

1605

Gavelkind and the other practices of Gaelic feudalism are banned.

The Government declares all Irish people are subject to the Crown alone.

Hugh Montgomery and James Hamilton are granted confiscated lands in Ulster.

Attendance at Protestant services is made compulsory.

Jesuits and other Roman Catholic priests are proscribed.

The Catholic gentry of the traditionally pro-English counties around Dublin object to the new religious edicts.

1606

The Brehon law code is formally abolished.

The Franciscans found St Anthony's College at Louvain in Belgium.

1607

The flight of the Earls – Hugh O'Neill, Rory O'Donnell and other
Ulster lords flee Ireland for Spain. Large areas of the six Ulster
counties are confiscated.

1608

A Government survey of confiscated Ulster lands is initiated.
Sir Caher O'Doherty of Inishowen rebels; he is killed and his estates
forfeited.

1609

Some 500,000 acres in Ulster are made available for settlement.

1610

The City of London undertakes to plant colonies in the area around
Derry. Hugh Montgomery and James Hamilton plant the Ards and
Clandeboye.
Barnabe Rich publishes *A New Description of Ireland*.

1611

By now there are almost 5,000 English settlers planted in Munster.
John Speed's publishes a picture map of Dublin.

1612

The first borough of the Ulster plantation is founded at Dungannon.
Cornelius O'Devany, Bishop of Down, is executed for treason.

1613

James I calls a Parliament in Dublin. Londonderry and Belfast are
chartered.
The first national convocation of the Irish Church is held in Dublin.

1614

There are 3,000 Irish soldiers and 300 priests living in the territories
of the King of Spain.
Building work begins on the Crawfordsburn Inn, Co. Down, reputedly
the oldest hotel in Ireland.
The death of 'Black Tom' Butler, the Tenth Earl of Ormond and the
main Irish supporter of Elizabeth I.

1615

The Dublin Parliament of James I is dissolved.

The Church of Ireland adopts the Confession of Faith.

The tomb of Sir Francis Chichester and his wife is erected in St Nicholas's Church, Carrickfergus.

1616

Hugh O'Neill, Earl of Tyrone, dies in Rome.

1617

The fortified mansion of Portumna, Co. Galway, is completed.

Fynes Moryson publishes *The Itinerary*, which includes an account of his Irish travels.

1618

Donal Cam O'Sullivan Beare murdered in Spain by English agents.

The walls of Derry completed.

1619

Commissioners are appointed for the plantation of Longford.

1620

Richard Boyle receives the title of Earl of Cork.

Luke Gernon publishes *The Discoverie of Ireland*.

1621

Further plantations in the Irish Midlands are authorised.

Custom House and a new wharf built in Dublin.

1622

The English population of the Ulster plantations now numbers about 29,500.

1623

The pamphlet 'Advertisements for Ireland' comments that Ulster planters prefer Irish tenants as they are willing to pay higher rents.

c1624

A Jacobean mansion is added to Donegal Castle by Sir Basil Brooke.

1625

The accession of Charles I. James Ussher is appointed Archbishop of
  Armagh.

1626

King Charles I offers his subjects 26 Graces (concessions) in return
  for subsidies to finance his army. Protestant bishops condemn the
  administration's tolerance of Catholicism.
The Munster fisheries are worth 29,000 pounds, mainly due to an
  abundance of pilchards.
The Franciscan, Michael O'Clery, returns to Ireland from Louvain,
  with the mission to collect old Irish manuscripts.

1627

The offer of the Graces causes a confrontation between the Dublin
  administration and Irish Protestants.

1628

Charles I grants 51 Graces for subsidies.
Ulster planters are permitted to place Irish tenants on part of their lands.
Michael O'Clery compiles *The Martyrology of Donegal*.

1629

Attempts to close Catholic churches and ban public services cause
  riots in Dublin.
The Provost of Trinity College bans all undergraduate plays.

1631

Algerian pirates sack the town of Baltimore and kidnap its
  inhabitants.

1632

Irish Catholics pay 20,000 pounds in subsidies to Charles I.
The pilgrimage site of St Patrick's Purgatory on Lough Derg is
  destroyed by the local Protestant bishop.
Stafford's *Pacata Hibernia*, an account of the Sir George Carew's
  campaigns in Munster, is published.

1633

Thomas Wentworth, the Earl of Strafford, is appointed Lord Deputy.

Edmund Spenser's *View of the Present State of Ireland* is published
  posthumously.
The Protestant cathedral at Londonderry is completed.

1634

The dispute between the Archbishoprics of Armagh and Dublin over
  primacy is decided in favour of Armagh.

c1634

Geoffrey Keating completes his *History of Ireland*, the first cohesive
  account written in the Irish language.

1635

The Crown confirms its title to land in Roscommon, Sligo and Mayo.
Thomas Wentworth provides open spaces on Stephen's Green and
  College Green so Dubliners can have a place to walk.
Licensing laws are introduced to regulate Dublin's taverns.
Michael O'Cleary, assisted by three other historians, compiles *The
  Annals of the Four Masters* – a chronology of Irish history from
  Gaelic sources.

1636

The Crown confirms its title to land in Galway.
Edward Bryce, a leading Ulster Protestant, is sentenced to perpetual
  silence after a dispute with Church of Ireland bishops.

1637

Ireland's first professional theatre, the New Theatre, opens in Dublin.

1638

Wentworth arrests Lord Chancellor Loftus.

1639

The 'Black Oath' of conformity is imposed on Ulster Protestants by
  Wentworth.

1640

War begins in Scotland. Wentworth raises an Irish army to support Charles
  I. He is accused of high treason by the 'Long Parliament' in England.

1641

Thomas Wentworth is executed by the English Parliament.

Patrick Darcey argues for the independent authority of the Irish Parliament.

Rebellion breaks out amongst the native Irish population of Ulster. Protestants are massacred at Portadown, Blackwatertown and other plantation settlements. The rebellion spreads. Old English landowners throughout Ireland take up arms in the Catholic cause. James, Earl of Ormond, assumes control of the Royalist forces in Ireland.

Catholics still own 59% of Irish land at this date.

1642

Fighting and massacres of Protestants continue.

Sir Phelim O'Neill fails to capture Drogheda after a three-month siege.

The 'Confederation of Kilkenny' is formed by Catholic leaders. Owen Roe O'Neill arrives in Ireland and is appointed leader of the Irish army in Ulster.

An army of Scottish Protestants under Robert Monro lands at Carrickfergus.

Father Luke Wadding is appointed Papal representative to the Confederation of Kilkenny.

The first Irish Presbytery is opened in Carrickfergus by Scottish soldiers – comprises four elders and five ministers.

1643

Ormond, on behalf of the Royalist Party in Ireland, signs a one-year truce with the Confederation of Kilkenny. Charles I appoints Ormond, Lord Lieutenant.

In Ulster, Owen Roe O'Neill defeats the Scottish army at Charlemont, Co. Armagh, but afterwards he is forced to retreat into Connaught.

Derryhivenny Castle, Co. Galway, is erected by the O'Maddens (thought to be the last tower house built in Ireland).

1644

The Solemn League and Covenant is taken by Monro's army. The Covenant becomes general amongst Ulster Protestants.

1645

Papal Envoy Rinuccini is sent from Rome to the Confederation of
Kilkenny.

1646

The Confederation of Kilkenny and Ormond formally make peace –
Rinuccini condemns the agreement.
Monro is defeated by Owen Roe O'Neill at the Battle of Benburb.

1647

An English Parliamentary army of 2,000 men is sent to Ireland.
Ormond surrenders Dublin to the Parliamentary force and leaves
Ireland. The Confederation army in Leinster is defeated at Dungan's
Hill, Co. Meath. Lord Inchiquin, leading the Parliament forces in
Munster, sacks Cashel and defeats a Confederation army at
Knockanuss.

1648

Lord Inchiquin switches allegiance to the Royalists and signs a truce
with the Confederation.
Rinuccini alienates Catholic leaders by his refusal to make peace with
the Royalists and flees to Galway.
The Confederation of Kilkenny holds its final meeting.

1649

Charles I is executed in London. Royalists capture Drogheda and
Dundalk.
The Royalists are defeated by the Parliamentary army outside Dublin
at the Battle of Rathmines.
Oliver Cromwell arrives in Dublin. Drogheda is stormed and its
inhabitants massacred on Cromwell's orders.
Owen Roe O'Neill, the leader of the Ulster Catholic forces, dies.

1650

Cromwell captures Kilkenny and Clonmel, then returns to England
leaving General Ireton in command.
Confederation forces in Ulster are routed at Scarriffhollis. Athlone,
Carlow and Waterford surrender to Parliament.
Ormond, Inchiquin and other leading Royalists leave for France.

1651

Limerick surrenders to Parliament.

The Navigation Act restricts Irish maritime trade to English ships
  only.

1652

Supporters of the Confederation in Leinster surrender under the
  'Articles of Kilkenny'.

Galway, the last major Royalist stronghold in Ireland,
  surrenders.

The 'Act for the Settling of Ireland' defines punishments for the
  population – including forfeiture of estates and transplantation to
  Clare and Connacht.

1653

Inisboffin Island, the last Royalist garrison in the British Isles,
  surrenders.

Thousands of destitute and vagrant Irish are rounded up and shipped
  to the West Indies.

Parliament declares the Irish Rebellion at an end.

1654

The Down Survey lists and allocates forfeited lands.

Transplantations of the Irish to Connaught begin; the estates they
  leave behind are given to adventurers or to Cromwell's soldiers in
  lieu of wages.

The celebration of Christmas is forbidden.

1655

The transplantation and expulsion of Catholics gathers pace – Dublin
  and Galway are cleared.

Easter celebrations are forbidden.

1656

Archbishop James Ussher (born 1581) of Armagh dies.

The Archbishop was a noted Biblical scholar who had fixed the date
  for God's creation of the world at 4004 BC.

 His book collection is later used to start the Trinity College Library in
  Dublin.

1657

The Settlement Act comes into being 'for the assuming, confirming
and settling of lands in Ireland'. Further harsh legislation is enacted
against suspected Catholics.

Erasmus Smith founds five elementary and five grammar schools.

1658

Oliver Cromwell dies in England.

1659

Army officers seize Dublin Castle in attempt to restore the authority
of the English Parliament.

1660

Charles II is restored to the throne in England and proclaimed King in
Ireland on 14 May.

A new Navigation Act restores Irish maritime rights.

1661

The Irish Parliament, closed by Cromwell, is restored.

James Butler is created Duke of Ormond and appointed Lord Lieutenant.

The Church of Ireland is re-established.

1662

The Settlement Act of provides for restitution of unfairly confiscated
properties, including those of some Catholics.

The English Parliament forbids the export of Irish wool.

Foreign Protestants are encouraged to settle in Ireland.

1663

Colonel Blood's planned rising of Cromwellian planters is foiled. The
Cattle Act of the English Parliament restricts Irish cattle exports and
trade with the colonies.

1664

Around this date over 74% of Irish exports are to England.

1665

Smithfield Market, Dublin, is founded for the sale of feed and
livestock.

1666

The Act of Uniformity restricts religious, teaching and official
 positions to members of the Church of Ireland.

1667

England and Scotland ban imports of Irish livestock.
The College of Physicians is founded.

1668

Around 12,000 Irish people have now been transported to the West Indies.
The barn-style Middle Church at Upper Ballinderry, Co. Antrim, is
 consecrated.

1669

George Fox, founder of the Quaker faith, visits Ireland.

c1670

Jews from the Canary Islands flee the Inquisition and settle in Dublin.

1671

The second Navigation Act restricts direct imports from the colonies
 to Ireland.

1672

Regium Donum grants to Presbyterian ministers are initiated.

1673

The Test Act demands that all office holders take Church of Ireland
 sacraments.
The first chart of Dublin Bay is drawn by Sir Bernard de Gomme.

1674

The death of the Earl of Inchiquin.

c1675

Hoare's Bank, the first in Ireland, opens in Cork.

1676

Around this time, unfortified houses with Dutch gables like Eyrecourt,
 Co. Galway, and Beaulieu, Co. Louth, are built.

1677

The Duke of Ormond is sworn in for a second term as Lord
Lieutenant. Charles Fort is built to protect Kinsale Harbour
(architect, Sir William Robinson).

1678

Archbishop Talbot of Dublin arrested after Titus Oates accuses him of
involvement in a 'Popish Plot'.

1679

Oliver Plunkett, Archbishop of Armagh, is arrested on suspicion of
involvement in a 'Popish Plot'.

1680

Work begins on the Royal Hospital, Kilmainham, Dublin's first
classical building.
Three members of the audience are killed when the galleries of the
Smock Alley Theatre collapse during a performance of Ben
Johnson's *Bartholomew Fair*.

1681

Oliver Plunkett is convicted of treason on false evidence and
executed.

1682

The 'Long Bridge', linking Belfast to the Down side of the River
Lagan, is built at a cost of 12,000 pounds.
Richard Southwell builds the Almshouses at Kinsale, Co. Cork.

1684

The Dublin Philosophical Society is founded by William Molyneux.
The first public dissection of a human corpse in Ireland takes place.

1685

James II, widely considered to be sympathetic to Catholics, succeeds
to the throne of England and Ireland.
The first complete Old Testament in Irish is published in London (the
translation was initiated in 1629 by William Bedel).
William Petty's Map of Ireland is published.

1686

The Earl of Tyrconnell is appointed Lieutenant General of the army.
The Government directs the Exchequer to pay Catholic bishops and
archbishops.
Jonathan Swift graduates from Trinity College.

1687

Tyrconnell is sworn in as Lord Deputy.
Public lighting is introduced in Dublin.

1688

Apprentice Boys close the gates of Derry against Royal troops.
William of Orange lands in England. James II flees to France.
The percentage of land owned by Catholics has shrunk to 22%.

1689

William of Orange and his wife Mary ascend the English throne.
James II arrives in Ireland seeking help to reclaim his throne. James
 II's army fails to capture Londonderry after a siege of 15 weeks.
Marshall Schomberg lands near Carrickfergus with a large Williamite
 army.

1690

French troops arrive to support James II.
William of Orange lands in Ireland at Carrickfergus.
The army of James II is defeated at the Battle of the Boyne (July I).
 James departs from Ireland three days later.
Patrick Sarsfield attacks the Williamite siege train in a daring cavalry
 raid near Limerick (Sarsfield's Ride). William advances on Limerick
 but fails to take the city – he returns to England in September.
The Duke of Marlborough captures Cork and the forts protecting
 Kinsale.

1691

A French army under the Marquis de St Ruth sails into Limerick. At
 the Battle of Aughrim, General Ginkel's Williamite army defeats the
 French and Irish forces led by St Ruth, who is killed (July 12).
Limerick is surrounded and besieged by the Williamites (25 August–
 24 September).

The Treaty of Limerick is signed, allowing the defeated supporters of
   James II to leave Ireland and promising religious tolerance for
   Catholics. Sarsfield and other Irish officers depart for France,
   becoming known in later years as the 'Wild Geese'.

1692

Over 1,000,000 acres of land belonging to Irish supporters of James II
   are confiscated.
The Irish Parliament, now completely Protestant, meets for a short
   session.

1693

Patrick Sarsfield dies after being wounded at the Battle of Landen.

1694

William becomes the sole monarch of England and Ireland after his
   wife Mary dies.

1695

The beginning of the era of the Anglo-Irish Ascendancy. The Irish
   Parliament meets and passes acts which contravene the promise of
   tolerance in the Treaty of Limerick.
Penal Laws are passed forbidding Catholics their rights to bear arms
   and to educate their children or open schools.

1696

Duties on Irish linen entering England are removed in order to
   encourage the industry.

1697

Further Penal Laws ban burials in Catholic graveyards and exile all
   Catholic clergy.
Two new parishes formed on north side of the River Liffey to cater for
   Dublin's expanding population.

1698

Catholic clergy are expelled en masse.
William Molyneux's tract *Case of Ireland being Bound by Acts of
   Parliament in England Stated* is condemned in Westminster.

1699

Duties and restrictions are imposed on Irish wool exports to England.

Molly Malone, the subject of the famous Dublin street song, is reputed
  to have died in this year.

1700

The population of Ireland is now about 2,000,000.

In the aftermath of the Williamite wars, the Government holds over
  600,000 acres of confiscated Irish land.

1701

Work begins on Marsh's Library, Dublin.

1702

The death of William of Orange. His successor, Queen Anne, is a strict
  Anglican.

The Huguenot settlement at Portarlington, founded in 1667, is now a
  thriving market town.

1703

The town walls of Cork are demolished to allow for the city's expansion.

The first Irish newspaper begins publication (*Pue's Imperial
  Occurrences*).

1704

Yet more Penal Laws are imposed – Catholic ownership and tenancy
  of land is restricted and Dissenters and Catholics are excluded from
  public office.

The Bible is printed in Ireland for the first time by James Blow (Belfast).

Jonathan Swift publishes *The Tale of a Tub*.

1705

British colonies in America are opened to direct trade in linen with
  Ireland.

1706

Following the plantations and confiscations during the previous
  century only 18% of Irish land now remains in Catholic
  ownership.

1707

George Farquhar writes *The Beaux' Strategem* , which is considered to
  be the last great Restoration comedy.

1708

Cork repeals by-laws which are hindering the activities of the city's
  Catholic merchants.

1709

A Palatine settlement is established in Rathkeale (Limerick).
Sir Richard Steele publishes the first edition of *The Tatler* in London
  (ends 1711).

1710

Smithwick's, Ireland's oldest surviving brewery, opens in Kilkenny.
The last recorded wolf in Ireland is shot.
The philosopher, George Berkeley, publishes *A Treatise Concerning
  Human Knowledge.*
Jonathan Swift begins writing his *Journal to Stella*, an account of his
  life in London.

1711

The commencement of an era of recurrent warfare between tenants
  and landlords which lasts nearly two centuries.
In Connacht, the expropriation of land for pasture leads to the
  activities of the Houghers, who maim and slaughter thousands of
  sheep and cattle.
The Linen Board is established to help promote the linen industry.
The Medical School at Trinity College opens.

1712

Building work begins on the Trinity College Library (architect,
  Thomas Burgh).

1713

Jonathan Swift becomes Dean of St Patrick's Cathedral.

1714

The accession of George I, the first Hanoverian King.

1715
George I promises better treatment for dissenting Protestants.

c1716
A series of bad harvests causes great distress in Irish rural areas.

1717
The population of Ireland approaches 3,000,000.

1718
Ulster Scots emigrate in large numbers to the American colonies.
The Charitable Infirmary, Ireland's oldest hospital, is opened at Cork
  Street, Dublin (later moved to Jervis Street).

1719
The Toleration Act exempts Dissenting Protestants from the penalties
  imposed on Roman Catholics.
The Dublin Evening Chronicle is published for the first time.

1720
The Declaratory Act (Sixth of George I) lays down the supremacy of
  the English Parliament over the Irish Parliament.

1721
Ireland is excluded from East India trade, except through British ports.

1722
William Wood purchases the exclusive right to mint Irish coinage for
  14 years from the Duchess of Kendal, mistress of George I.
Work starts on Castletown House, Celbridge, Co. Kildare.

1723
Parliament condemns Wood's patent.

1724
The dispute about 'Wood's farthings' provokes Jonathan Swift to write
  The Drapier's Letters.
Melodies by the Irish harpist, Turlough Carolan, are published for the
  first time.

1726

The Presbytery of Antrim is established by non-subscribing
   Presbyterians.

The Quaker School at Ballitore, Co. Kildare, opens. The orator,
   Edmund Burke, will become its most famous pupil.

Jonathan Swift publishes *Gulliver's Travels*.

The death of Egan O'Rahilly (born 1670), Munster poet and author of 'Gile
   na Gile' (Brightness of Brightness) and many other Gaelic lyric poems.

1727

Thelkeld publishes *A Treatise on Irish Plants*.

The death of Samuel-Louis Crommellin, the Huguenot refugee who
   pioneered the Ulster linen industry.

1728

A new Act removes the franchise from Catholics. Catholics are
   forbidden to practise as solicitors.

The death of Stella (Esther Johnson), friend of Jonathan Swift and
   subject of his poem 'On Stella's Birthday'.

1729

A new wave of Ulster Scots emigrates to the American colonies.

The foundation stone is laid for the Parliament Building in College Green,
   Dublin (architect, Edward Lovett Pearce) – now the Bank of Ireland.

Jonathan Swift publishes *A Modest Proposal*, satirising the treatment
   of Dublin's poor.

1730

The potato is Ireland's staple diet for about three months of the year.

Building starts on Bellamont Forest, Cavan, one of the earliest
   Palladian houses in Ireland (architect, E. L. Pearce).

1731

The Irish Parliament meets in the new College Green building for the
   first time.

Thomas Molyneux founds the Dublin Society for Promoting
   Husbandry, Manufacturing and other Useful Arts.

Work starts on Powerscourt House, Co. Wicklow (architect, Richard
   Castle).

1733

The Government prohibits Irish trade with the West Indies.

The Charter Schools Movement is established to promote Church of
  Ireland education.

Dr Steeven's Hospital opens in Dublin.

1734

The philosopher, George Berkeley, is appointed to the Bishopric of
  Cloyne.

1735

George Berkeley publishes the first volume of *Queerist* (the third and
  final volume is published in 1737).

1736

A linen cambric factory is opened in Dundalk by the Huguenot A. de
  Joncourt.

Ireland's first daily paper, *The Dublin Daily Advertiser,* is published
  for the first time.

1737

The first issue of Ireland's oldest surviving newspaper is published –
  The Belfast Newletter.

1738

The death of Turlough Carolan (born 1670), Irish harpist.

1739

The Francini brothers create the stucco ceilings at Carton House,
  Kildare.

1740

There is a severe famine after a particularly harsh winter kills off
  livestock and destroys crops.

The Irish actress, Peg Woffington, performs in Covent Garden,
  London, to great acclaim.

c1740

The introduction of the first steam engines.

1741

The famine worsens after a second bad winter.
Newry is joined to Lough Neagh by Ireland's first canal.

1742

Handel's 'Messiah' is performed for the first time at the New Music
  Hall, Fishamble Street, Dublin (13 April). The massed choirs of St
  Patrick's and Christchurch Cathedrals participate, with takings being
  donated to local charities.
Work begins on Russborough House, Wicklow (architect, Richard
  Cassels).

c1743

The Dublin Society founds its famous Drawing Schools and takes
  over an existing school run by the artist, Robert West.

1744

Lord Lieutenant Chesterfield states 'the poor people of Ireland are
  used worse than negroes'.

1745

Some 4,000 Irishmen fight for the French army against British and
  Dutch forces at the Battle of Fontenoy.
Dr Bartholomew Mosse – 'man-midwife' – opens Ireland's first
  maternity hospital in George's Lane, Dublin.
Work begins on Leinster House (architect, Richard Cassels), which
  becomes the home of the Irish Parliament after 1924.
The death of Jonathan Swift (born 1667), clergyman, satirist and
  commentator.

1746

Irish Parliament bans marriage between Catholics and Protestants.

1747

John Wesley, the founder of Methodism, visits Ireland. He preaches at
  St Mary's Church, Dublin.

1748

France harbours a large number of clergy fleeing the Penal Laws –
  there are 39 Irish priests in the Gironde region alone.

1749

Work begins on St Patrick's Hospital for 'idiots and lunatics', paid for
by funds bequeathed by Jonathan Swift.

1750

Some 300,000 cattle are slaughtered annually in Cork for the export
trade. In the last 40 years, Cork has built an Exchange, a Customs
House, a Corn Market and a new cathedral.

1751

Work begins on the Rotunda Hospital, Dublin. Reputably Europe's
oldest custom-built maternity hospital (architect, Richard Cassels), it
opens in 1757.
The rebuilding of Essex Bridge, Dublin, on a cofferdam, is completed
(architect, William Semple).

1752

The Gregorian Calendar replaces the Julian Calendar.
A regular coach service between Dublin and Belfast is opened.
The building of the West Front of Trinity College, Dublin, begins.
The first steeplechase is run between the church at Buttevant, Cork,
and 'the spire of the St Leger Church' (Doneraile).

1753

'Money Crisis' – the Irish Parliament clashes with the Dublin Castle
administration when it wants to pay off the national debt with
surplus revenue.
A Delamain delphware factory is opened in Dublin (closes 1769).
The death of George Berkeley (born 1685), philosopher and cleric.

1754

The Brown Linen Hall is opened in Belfast.

1755

The population of Belfast is about 7,500.

1756

Work begins on the Grand Canal, linking Dublin to the River Barrow. By
1805, the canal will have been extended to join the Shannon waterway.
St John's Square, Limerick is completed.

1757

The Wide Street Commission is formed, which oversees the planning
and laying out of Georgian Dublin.

1758

Restrictions on the importing of Irish cattle and beef into England and
Scotland are lifted. This encourages landlords to take over common
land and increase pasturage.

1759

Arthur Guinness acquires a semi-derelict brewery at St James's Gate
from Mark Rainsford on a 9,000-year lease at 45 pounds per annum.
Work begins on the Provost's House, Trinity College, Dublin
(architect, John Smyth).

1760

The Catholic Committee is formed in Dublin.
The French raid Belfast Lough and occupy Carrickfergus Castle for
several days.
The death of Peg Woffington (born 1718), the greatest Irish actress of
her era.

1761

Deep unrest amongst Irish peasantry leads to the emergence of the
Whiteboy Agrarian Movement in Munster.
Edmund Burke is appointed assistant to W.G. Hamilton, chief
secretary of Ireland.

1762

Merrion Square is laid out, marking the beginning of the modern city
of Dublin.
The first important Irish neoclassical house is built in Dublin. Today it
is the Municipal Gallery of Art (architect, William Chambers) in
Parnell Square.
Oliver Goldsmith publishes *The Chinese Letters.*

1763

The Whiteboy Agrarian Movement becomes active in Ulster.
The first issue of *The Freeman's Journal* is published.

1764

Work begins on the Rotunda Rooms at the north end of Sackville
  Street, Dublin.
The Earl of Mornington (father of the Duke of Wellington) is
  appointed first Professor of Music at Trinity College, Dublin.

1765

The English Government purchases the Isle of Man (chief depot for
  Irish smugglers) from the Duke of Athol. Henceforth many illegal
  exports are shipped to Guernsey.
Work begins on the Limerick Custom House (architect, Davis
  Duckart).

1766

The Tumultuous Risings Act gives the Government special powers to
  deal with the Whiteboys.
Oliver Goldsmith publishes *The Vicar of Wakefield*.

1767

The water-powered mill at Slane, Co. Meath, is completed at a cost of
  20,000 pounds.
Building work begins on Castletown Cox, Co. Kilkenny, one of the
  last Palladian houses built in Ireland (architect, Davis Duckart).

1768

The term of the Irish Parliament is limited to eight years (Octennial
  Act).

1769

Steelboy or Hearts of Steel Movement becomes active in Ulster. The
  Cork Butter Market is established.
Building is completed on the Marino Casino – a neoclassic villa near
  Dublin (architect, William Chambers).

1770

There are agrarian riots in Ulster. Five farmers are killed when the
  army opens fire on Steelboy protestors in Belfast.
The Assembly Rooms in Limerick are built.
Oliver Goldsmith publishes *The Deserted Village*.

1771

Benjamin Franklin visits Ireland.

Peter Corcoran becomes the first Irish Bareknuckle Boxing Champion
of England when he beats Bill Darts in a 'fixed' fight.

1772

The Steelboys Act gives emergency powers to the authorities in Ulster.

Catholics are permitted to lease bogland.

1773

The 'Penny Post' is introduced in Dublin.

British soldiers murder Art O'Leary near Millstreet for his horse. His
wife writes the Gaelic poem 'The Lament for Art O'Leary'.

Mayoralty House, Cork, later Mercy Hospital, is completed (architect,
Davis Duckart).

Oliver Goldsmith's *She Stoops to Conquer* is staged for the first time.

1774

The Enabling Act permits Catholics to swear allegiance to the King.

The White Linen Hall is opened in Donegall Square, Belfast.

Oliver Goldsmith (born 1728) dies.

1775

Henry Flood resigns as leader of the opposition Patriot Party in the
Irish Parliament after he accepts Government office. Henry Grattan
becomes new leader of the Patriot Party.

Two Whiteboys are executed following agrarian disturbances in Co.
Wexford.

The American War of Independence begins.

Richard Brinsley Sheridan's *The Rivals* is staged for the first time.

Nathaniel Hone paints 'The Conjuror'.

1776

The Ranelagh Gardens open, rapidly becoming the centre of Dublin's
social life.

1777

The Presentation Sisters is founded in Cork by Nano Nagle.

Richard Brinsley Sheridan's *School for Scandal* staged for the first
time.

1778

The threat of foreign invasion encourages Protestants to form
   Volunteer Companies in Belfast and Dublin. By the end of the year
   40,000 Volunteers are enlisted.
The American privateer, John Paul Jones, raids Belfast Lough.
Gardiner's Catholic Relief Act restores the right to take long-term
   leases and inherit land.

1779

Irish Volunteers celebrate William of Orange's birthday by parading in
   College Green with placards demanding free trade.
In New York, the first St Patrick's Day Parade takes place.

1780

The potato is now the staple diet for most of the rural population of
   Ireland.
Ireland is allowed free trade with the colonies.
Grattan proposes legislative independence for Ireland (rejected).
Sacramental tests for Dissenting protestants are repealed.
Arthur Young publishes *A Tour in Ireland*.

c 1780

Brian Merriman writes the Irish poem 'Cúirt an Mheán Oíche' (the
   Midnight Court).

1781

Volunteers meet in Armagh and demand the reform of the
   Administration and independence for the Irish Parliament.
Work begins in Dublin on the new Customs House (architect, James
   Gandon; sculptures of riverine heads and the Arms of Ireland,
   Edward Smyth).

1782

The Ulster Volunteers Convention in Dungannon calls for legislative
   independence and the repeal of all Penal Laws.
The British Parliament repeals the Sixth of George I Declaratory
   Act, conceding the independence of the Irish Parliament. Poyning's
   Law is amended in favour of the Irish Parliament (Yelverton's Act)
   and independence of the Irish Judiciary is established (Forbe's
   Act).

Gardiner's second and third Catholic Relief Acts restore property
  rights and permit Catholic schools.
In Dublin, the Kildare Street Club is founded.

1783

The Renunciation Act is passed by the new Whig Government in
  Westminster, recognising the right of the Irish Parliament to legislate
  independently. The Volunteer Movement presents a bill for the
  reform of Parliament – it is rejected.
The Penrose family open a glass factory in Waterford.
The Bank of Ireland – the country's first joint stock bank – is
  established in Dublin.

1784

The Belfast Volunteers invite Catholics to join their ranks and help
  fund the erection of St Mary's Chapel.
The Irish Government makes provision for a postal service.
The 'Most Illustrious Order of St Patrick' is inaugurated in St
  Patrick's Cathedral.
The deaths of Nathaniel Hone, the elder (born 1718), artist, and
  George Barret (born 1732), landscape artist.

1785

The population of Ireland has doubled since 1700 and now stands at
  about 4,000,000.
Grattan's attempt to win free trade between Ireland and England fails
  when he rejects Prime Minister Pitt's amendments to his proposals.
Ulster Catholics found a new agrarian secret society called the
  Defenders – it spreads across Ireland over the next few years.
The Irish Academy is founded (becomes the Royal Irish Academy in 1786).
Slane Castle, Meath, is gothicised (architect, Thomas Wyatt).
The death of Davis Duckart, Sardinian architect. He was the last great
  exponent of the Palladian style in Ireland.

1786

Work begins on Four Courts, Dublin (architect, James Gandon).

1787

Continued agrarian unrest leads to the introduction of the British Riot
  Act (the so-called 'Whiteboys Act').

1788

The madness of George III causes a constitutional crisis in England.

1789

The Irish Parliament votes for the Prince of Wales as Regent of
  Ireland.
John Wesley visits Ireland for the twentieth and final time.
The Whig Club is formed by Henry Grattan and other patriots.
Armagh Observatory is founded.
Patrick's Bridge is opened in Cork. It joins the newly built Patrick
  Street to the northern slopes of the city.

1790

Edmund Burke publishes *Reflections on the Revolution in France.*
The death of Robert West, greatest of the 18th-century Irish stucco
  artists.

1791

Samuel McTier and Robert Simms found the Society of United
  Irishmen in Belfast (14 October). The Society of United Irishmen of
  Dublin is established, with Napper Tandy as its first secretary (9
  November).
Irish Catholics petition the King for relief from oppression.
William Ritchie builds Belfast's first important shipyard. The
  population of the town is now over 18,000.
Daly's Club, Dublin, is renovated into a sumptuous gambling house.
Wolfe Tone publishes *Argument on Behalf of the Catholics of Ireland.*

1792

The Belfast Volunteers Convention votes for immediate Catholic
  emancipation.
Langrishe's Catholic Relief Act allows the practise of law and
  removes the legal ban on intermarriage.
A Catholic convention in Dublin (the 'Back Lane' Parliament) decides
  to send a delegation to the King.
Wolfe Tone is appointed secretary of the Catholic Committee.
A harp festival is held in Belfast. It inspires Edward Bunting to begin
  collecting the Irish airs later published in *Ancient Irish Music*
  (Volumes 1, 2 and 3 in 1802, 1809 and 1840 respectively).
The first of Malton's prints of Dublin are published (series ends 1799).

1793

Wolfe Tone and a delegation of Catholics meet the King. Napper
   Tandy flees Ireland when he is accused of being a Defender.

The Militia Act provides for local militias to be raised throughout
   Ireland.

Government forces kill over 80 agrarian protestors at Taghmon, Co.
   Wexford.

Hobart's Catholic Relief Act restores the vote and removes most
   remaining bars to Catholics, although higher State offices remain
   closed to them.

St Patrick's College, the first Catholic institution for higher studies, is
   founded in Carlow.

Castlecoole House, Fermanagh, is completed (architect, James Wyatt).

1794

Dublin United Irishmen are suppressed. Wolfe Tone meets with
   French agents in Dublin.

Catholics are enabled by law to attend Trinity College, Dublin.

1795

The United Irishmen turn themselves into a secret society dedicated to
   the military overthrow of English power. Wolfe Tone leaves for
   America.

Formation of the Orange Order in Loughall, Co. Armagh, after
   Presbyterians rout Catholic Defenders in the riot known as the
   'Battle of the Diamond'.

Grattan fails to obtain a further Catholic Relief Bill.

The seminary of the Royal College of St Patrick, Maynooth, opens.

Carlisle Bridge, Dublin is completed (architect, James Gandon).

Work begins on theKing's Inns, Dublin (architect, James Gandon).

The Royal Dublin Society establishes the National Botanic Gardens
   on 25 acres at Glasnevin, Dublin.

Maria Edgeworth publishes *Letters for Literary Ladies*.

1796

Wolfe Tone arrives in France to seek aid for a rising.

Lord Edward Fitzgerald joins the United Irishmen.

The Government suspends the Insurrection Act and implements
   Habeas Corpus.

The leaders of the Belfast United Irishmen are arrested.

Landlords are encouraged to raise a corps of armed Protestant Yeomen.

Admiral Hoche's French invasion fleet – accompanied by Wolfe Tone – fails to land due to storms.

The Orange Order holds its first Twelfth of July March in Lurgan.

1797

Authorities impose Martial Law and proclaim the United Irishmen.

The Catholic areas of Ulster are suppressed by General Lake.

United Irishman, William Orr, is executed in Carrickfergus.

Henry Grattan retires from Parliament. Edmund Burke (born 1729), orator and political philosopher, dies in England.

1798

A rising of United Irishmen is planned for May 23. Leinster United Irishmen leaders are arrested in Dublin (March). Lord Edward Fitzgerald (born 1763) is arrested in Dublin and dies of wounds received (4 June). The rising in the counties around Dublin fails. There are minor engagements at Naas, Prosperous, Kilcullen and elsewhere.

In Wexford, massacres of Catholics at Dunlavin and Carnew panic the population. Near Harrow, a small force of local Catholics led by Father John Murphy clashes with a militia patrol – sparking an insurrection. Rebel forces camp at Vinegar Hill (29 May) and capture Wexford (1 June). Insurgent detachments defeated at Bunclody and New Ross. The main army routes the British at Tubberneering and advances north towards Dublin. At the Battle of Arklow, the Wexford army is decisively defeated and retreats back to Vinegar Hill. General Lake's army storms Vinegar Hill and Wexford town is recaptured on the same day (31 June).

The Ulster Rising, predominantly Presbyterian, is confined to Counties Down and Antrim. The United Irish of Antrim are routed on 7 June by Government troops (their leader, Henry Joy McCracken, is executed in July). The 7000-strong Down United Irishmen army, which includes several thousand Catholics, is defeated at the Battle of Ballynahinch (13 June).

French forces under General Humbert land at Killalla, Mayo (August).

The Government garrison is routed in the 'Races of Castlebar'.
Humbert advances towards Dublin but finds little support and faces
a a much larger British army. He surrenders at Ballinamuck,
Longford (8 September). The capture of Killalla ends major
resistance in Ireland (23 September).

The French invasion fleet is defeated off the Donegal coast, losing
seven of its ten ships (10 October). Wolfe Tone (born 1763) is
captured in Lough Foyle. He cuts his throat on 12 November
when told he will be hung rather than shot as a soldier, and dies a
week later.

The Irish Parliament is suspended in the aftermath of the Rebellion.
Robert Stewart (Viscount Castlereagh) is appointed Chief Secretary.

The Newtown Quaker school, Waterford, is founded.

1799

Prime Minister Pitt proposes the Parliamentary Union of Ireland and
Great Britain. Castlereagh launches a campaign of bribery and
persuasion to secure the Union in the Irish Parliament.

Arthur Guinness turns the entire production of the St James's Gate
brewery over to porter (a dark sweet ale brewed from black malt).

1800

The last session of the Irish Parliament opens. After Castlereagh packs
it with pro-Union members, the Act of Union is carried on June 7.

Henry Grattan returns from retirement to oppose the Union.

Maria Edgeworth publishes *Castle Rackrent* anonymously. Thomas
Moore publishes his translation of *The Odes of Anacreon*.

Hugh Douglas Hamilton exhibits the painting *Cupid and Psyche*.

1801

The Union of Great Britain and Ireland, with a single Parliament in
London, is now a reality.

The Copyright Act stops Irish publishers pirating books.

Death of Michael Stapleton, stuccodore – plasterworks include Slane
Castle, Westport House and Belvedere House.

1802

Robert Emmet returns from France to plan a new insurrection.
Edmund Ignatius Rice opens his first school in Waterford.

1803

Robert Emmet marches towards Dublin Castle with about 100 unruly
   followers; Lord Kilwarden (the Lord Chief Justice) and his nephew
   are murdered by the mob. The army disperses the crowd and Emmet
   flees (23 July). Emmet is arrested (25 August), tried for treason and
   executed in Dublin (20 September). Thomas Russell, chief co-
   conspirator of this 1803 Rising, is arrested in Ulster and executed in
   Downpatrick (21 October). Michael Dwyer, fighting a guerilla war
   in Wicklow Mountains since the 1798 Rising, surrenders and is
   transported to Australia.

1804

Cork Street Fever Hospital, Dublin, is founded.
James Barry paints his 'Self Portrait'.

1805

The death of Brian Merriman (born c1747), Gaelic poet.

1806

Lady Morgan (Sydney Owenson) publishes *The Wild Irish Girl*.

1807

Thresher land agitation in Longford. Five Threshers are hanged for
   murdering an informer.
The death of Dennis Hempson, last of the traditional Irish harpists.

1808

The 'Veto controversy' arises over the Catholic Hierarchy's right to
   appoint bishops to vacant sees.
Edmund Ignatius Rice founds the Irish Christian Brothers, adapting
   the order's rules from those of the Presentation Sisters.
Work begins on Nelson's Pillar in Dublin (height from base to top of
   statue, 144 feet (44 metres).
Thomas Moore publishes the first volume of *Irish Melodies*, with
   music by Sir John Stevenson (tenth and final volume published in
   1843).

1809

The Catholic Committee re-established as the Catholic Board.

1810

Legislation is drafted to curb rural secret societies (the Unlawful Oaths Act).

1811

The Kish Lighthouse is erected in Dublin Bay.

Kildare Place Society founded to promote non-denominational free schools.

1812

The English poet, Percy Bysshe Shelley, arrives in Dublin to foment a revolution but he abandons his plans after two months and leaves Ireland.

Martello towers are erected to guard harbours and strategic coastlines against the French.

1813

Grattan's Relief Bill fails in the British House of Commons by four votes.

The first Twelfth of July sectarian riots take place in Belfast.

The largest meteorite recorded in Ireland, weighing 65 lbs (29 kg), lands in Co. Limerick.

1814

Chief Secretary Robert Peel establishes an Irish police force (popularly known as the 'Peelers').

Carlow Castle is blown up by a Dr Middleton to make room for a lunatic asylum.

Work begins on the General Post Office (GPO) building in Sackville Street, Dublin.

Belfast Academy is founded (it becomes Royal Belfast Academy in 1831).

1815

The Battle of Waterloo takes place. The end of the Napoleonic Wars brings about economic recession in agriculture and urban industry.

Daniel O'Connell kills John d'Esterre in a duel near Dublin.

Charles Bianconi launchs his first mail-car passenger route, from Clonmel to Cahir, Tipperary.

Mountjoy Square, Dublin, is completed.

Irish prize-fighter, Dan Donnelly, wins a famous victory over the
  Champion of England on the Curragh, Kildare.

1816
Famine and a typhus epidemic follow the failure of the potato crop.
Halfpenny Bridge is built in Dublin.
The death of Richard Brinsley Sheridan (born 1751), dramatist.

1817
The typhus epidemic kills at least 50,000 people.
The foundations of a new pier are laid at Kingstown, Co. Dublin.
  Kingstown becomes the main passenger terminal for Dublin.
Maria Edgeworth publishes *Ormond*.

1818
The Ulster Presbyterian Synod splits after the election of the Rev
  Henry Montgomery.
The first steamboat crossing of the Irish Sea is made by the *Rob Roy*.
William Carleton arrives in Dublin and soon embarks on a literary career.

1819
Sullivan and Scanlan are hanged for the 'Colleen Bawn' murder of
  Ellen Hanly in Limerick – their crime inspires several famous
  literary works.

1820
Ribbonmen disturbances in rural Connacht.
Completion of the Wellington Obelisk in the Phoenix Park, Dublin.
The Crow Street Theatre, Dublin, is closed down.
Henry Grattan (born 1756) dies in London.

1821
King George IV visits Ireland – the first visit by a British monarch
  since the flight of James II.
Seventeen people are burnt to death in Tipperary by Rockite rural
  terrorists.
The potato crop fails.
The Bank of Ireland's monopoly on banking is abolished, except
  within Dublin.
Dublin house prices are estimated to have fallen by 30% since 1800.

1822

Widespread famine and fever epidemics in rural areas.

Robert Stewart (Lord Castlereagh), the main instigator of the Act of Union, commits suicide.

Arthur Guinness II begins to brew Extra Strength Porter – the precursor of modern Guinness.

1823

Daniel O'Connell forms the Catholic Association to agitate for emancipation.

The harp is removed from Irish coinage.

1824

A UK Act allows free trade in manufactured articles between Ireland and England.

The Catholic Association introduces a subscription of one penny a month (the 'Catholic Rent').

Henry Cooke becomes Moderator of the Synod of Ulster.

William Rowan Hamilton develops the 'Theory of System of Rays' predicting conical refraction.

Charles Robert Maturin publishes *Melmoth the Wanderer*.

Bare knuckle boxer Jack Langan loses two epic contests with the English Champion, Tom Spring – at Worcester Racecourse (77 rounds) and Birdham Bridge (76 rounds).

1825

The UK House of Lords rejects a Bill granting Catholic emancipation.

The Pro-Cathedral (Catholic) in Marlborough Street, Dublin, is consecrated.

1826

Catholic Association candidate, Richard Powers, defeats Lord Beresford in the Waterford election.

The collapse of the weaving industry causes mass unemployment in the cities and riots in Dublin.

1827

Sir Jonah Barrington publishes the first volume of *Personal Sketches of His Own Times* (third and final volume in1832). Lady Morgan publishes *The O'Briens and the O'Flahertys*.

1828

The Catholic Association holds a series of parish meetings
simultaneously throughout Ireland.

Brunswick clubs are founded by Loyalistaristocrats in response to the
Emancipation Movement.

Daniel O'Connell wins the Clare by-election but cannot enter
Parliament because of the 'Oath of Supremacy'.

Dublin's first Catholic cemetery is opened at Golden Bridge.

Francis Danby paints *The Opening of the Seventh Seal* (now in the
National Gallery of Ireland).

1829

Catholic emancipation is granted by a Relief Act which allows
Catholics to enter Parliament, and to hold civil and military offices.

The property qualification is raised from two pounds to ten pounds in
an attempt to exclude Catholic voters.

O'Connell is informed his election is invalid because the Act is not
retrospective – he is re-elected unopposed to Clare.

John O'Donovan appointed to the Ordinance Survey of Ireland. His
notes and letters are to become a major historical source.

Gerald Griffin publishes *The Collegians* (inspired by the 'Colleen
Bawn' murder case).

1830

Daniel O'Connell takes his seat in the House of Commons.

The Dublin Zoo, the third oldest zoo in the world, is opened by the Dublin
Zoological Society.

The Black Church, Dublin, is completed (architect, John Semple).

William Carleton publishes *Traits and Stories of the Irish Peasantry*
(second series published in1833).

1831

The so-called 'tithe war' begins in Co. Kilkenny and spreads
throughout Leinster, culminating in the death of 17 policemen in a
riot at Carrishock, Kilkenny.

The National Education Board is founded.

Nine acres at Glasnevin, Dublin, are purchased for a Catholic
cemetery.

Samuel Lover publishes *Legends and Stories of Ireland*.

1832

The Irish Reform Act increases Irish seats in the House of Commons
from 100 to 105 and widens the franchise to include more
Catholics.

The Government suspends tithes in the face of rural agitation.

The cholera epidemic causes many deaths.

The Tarbert Lighthouse, guarding the Shannon approaches to
Limerick, is completed.

1833

The number of Church of Ireland dioceses is reduced from 22 to 12
dioceses.

The *Dublin University Magazine* is founded. It is noted for publishing
poems by James Clarence Mangan and Samuel Ferguson.

1834

Daniel O'Connell's motion on the Repeal of the Union is debated in
the UK House of Commons.

The most violent 'faction fight' of the century, at Ballyveigue, Co.
Kerry, claims two dozen lives.

Henry Cooke addresses a mass rally of Presbyterians at Hillsborough.
He forges an alliance with the Church of Ireland against Catholics.

The last sighting of a Great Auk in Ireland, at Waterford Harbour.

Ireland's first railway, between Dublin and Kingstown (Dun
Laoghaire), opens.

Jockey Pat Connolly wins the first of two Epsom Derby victories on
Plenipotentiary (wins on Coronation in 1841).

1835

The Lichfield House Agreement allies O'Connell's Irish party with the
Whigs and Radicals.

Thomas Drummond is appointed as Under Secretary of Ireland.

The report of a Royal Commission on Poverty reveals that labourers
live and work in appalling conditions.

The Association of Non-subscribing Presbyterians is formed.

Wellesley Bridge – now Sarsfield Bridge – is opened in Limerick
(architect, Alexander Nimmo).

Picturesque Sketches etc. is published, including reviews by the artists
George Petrie, Andrew Nicholl and Henry O'Neill.

1836

The Royal Irish Constabulary and the Dublin Metropolitan Police are
   established to replace local constabularies.
The Orange Order dissolves itself.
The Synod of Ulster makes subscription to the Westminster
   Confession of Faith obligatory.
The Ulster Bank is founded.
Francis Mahony publishes *The Reliques of Father Prout*.

1837

Queen Victoria ascends to the throne.
Lord Kingsborough, eccentric and scholar, dies after being imprisoned
   for debts incurred in printing his ten-volume *Antiquities of Mexico*,
   which purport to prove that ancient Hebrews colonised Central
   America.
The Irish composer, John Field, dies in Moscow.

1838

The English Poor Law is extended to Ireland. It establishes the
   notorious workhouse system.
Tithes are abolished and replaced by a less onerous fixed rent.
Father Theobald Matthew begins his temperance crusade in Cork.
Work starts on St Patrick's Roman Catholic Cathedral in Armagh
   (architect, Thomas Duff and after 1853, J.J. McCarthy).

1839

The 'Big Wind' causes destruction all over Ireland (6/7 January).
The first railway in Ulster begins operating.
Francis Beatty takes the first daguerreotype photograph in Ireland –
   probably of the Long Bridge, Belfast.

1840

Daniel O'Connell forms the Repeal Association. The first Repeal
   Association mass rally is held in Castlebar.
Dublin's first omnibus service is opened between the city centre and
   the southern suburbs of Clonskeagh, Sandymount and
   Rathfarnham.
The Ulster Synod and the Secessionist Synod merge to form the
   General Assembly of the Presbyterian Church in Ireland.

Father Theobald Mathew preaches in Dublin. By the end of the year,
   over 100,000 Dubliners have taken the Temperance Pledge.
Work begins on the Longford Roman Catholic Cathedral.
George Petrie issues *The Irish Penny Journal*.
Thomas Drummond, a respected and sympathetic Administrator of
   Ireland, dies.

1841

The first accurate census of Ireland records a population of 8,175,124.
The first photographic studio in Ireland is opened in the Rotunda
   Rooms, Dublin.
The building of St Mary's Cathedral, Killarney, commences (architect,
   A.W. N. Pugin).
The Cork Examiner newspaper is founded.
Charles Lever publishes *Charles O'Malley*.
The death of landscape painter, James Arthur O'Connor (born 1792).

1842

Daniel O'Connell serves as Mayor of Dublin.
Potato blight destroys the crop in the eastern United States.
First issue of *The Nation* published by Thomas Davis and the Young
   Ireland Movement.
Samuel Lover publishes *Handy Andy*, his best-known comic novel.

1843

A series of 'monster meetings' is held to press for the repeal of the
   Union, culminating in the rally at Tara attended by three quarters of
   a million people (15 August). The meeting planned for Clontarf on 8
   October is banned by the authorities. Daniel O'Connell cancels it
   and is arrested a week later on charges of conspiracy.
The world's largest reflecting telescope is cast for William Parsons,
   Earl of Rosse (begins operating at Birr Castle in 1845).
The earliest known photographic views of Dublin are taken by Fox Talbot.
Mucross House, Killarney, is built (architect, William Burn).
Michael William Balfe composes 'The Bohemian Girl'. Thomas Davis
   publishes *The Spirit of the Nation*, a collection of his best songs.

1844

Daniel O'Connell is convicted and spends three and a half months in
   prison before he is freed by the UK House of Lords.

The Charitable Donations and Bequests Board is established.

The 'funicular' railway between Kingstown and Dalkey opens
  (powered until 1854 by the rare 'atmospheric' system).

Sir William Rowan Hamilton defines the 'quaternions'.

Samuel Lover starts performing at 'Irish evenings' of songs, stories
  and recitations.

1845

Potato blight crosses the Atlantic and appears in England. It crosses to
  Wexford and Waterford (first newspaper report, 9 September). Half
  of the annual potato harvest is ruined (November). The Great
  Famine begins. Prime Minister Robert Peel orders corn and meal to
  be sent from the United States. A Relief Commission is set up under
  Edward Lucas.

The Bank of Ireland's monopoly in Dublin is abolished.

The Government provides for the establishment of Queen's Colleges
  in Cork, Galway and Belfast.

Maynooth College receives State funding for the first time.

The Geological Survey of Ireland begins (not completed until
  1887).

The velocipede, precursor of the bicycle, makes its first appearance in
  Ireland.

James Clarence Mangan publishes *Antholgia Germanica*. John
  O'Donovan publishes *A Grammar of the Irish Language*.

The death of Thomas Davis (born 1814), patriot and poet.

1846

Potato blight almost totally destroys the year's crop. The famine
  worsens.

Whig Government falls. Lord Russell's Tory Government halts food
  and relief works (re-instates them by end of year). The Central
  Relief Committee of the Society of Friends is set up to alleviate
  suffering.

Despite the famine, large quantities of grain are exported to pay the
  rents of absentee landlords.

Almost a third of a million destitute people are employed in public
  works (December).

In Mexico, the San Patricio battalion is formed from Irish deserters
  from the US army to fight in the war between Mexico and America.

The first Bewley's Café is opened in Dublin.

1847

The famine worsens after an exceptionally bad winter. Typhus epidemic kills tens of thousands. The Soup Kitchens Act provides financial assistance to local authorities to help them feed famine victims. However, the Act is withdrawn in September when funding relief becomes dependent on local rates and charitable donations.

The Poor Relief Act allows magistrates to extend help to the needy (excluding tenants holding more than a quarter acre). The potato crop is healthy but so few have been planted that the famine continues unabated (August).

The American packet boat *Stephen Whitney* sinks off the coast of Cork. This encourages the building of a lighthouse on the Fastnet Rock.

In Mexico, the San Patricio Battalion are overwhelmed at the Convent of Churubusco. The US army hangs 50 prisoners as deserters.

Daniel O'Connell (born 1775), the 'Liberator', dies in Genoa.

1848

The Famine continues. There are outbreaks of cholera and the potato harvest fails. The number of evictions rises. Famine victims on outdoor relief peak at almost 840,000 people (July).

John Mitchel breaks with *The Nation* and begins publishing the militant *United Irishman*.

The Government passes the Treason–Felony Act to deal with the Young Ireland revolutionaries. Events in Europe (the 'Year of Liberty') encourage an attempted rebellion by the Young Ireland Movement . John Mitchel is arrested and sentenced to 14 years' transportation to Australia.

There is an abortive rising led by William Smith O'Brien. He besieges police in the cottage of the Widow McCormack. Afterwards O'Brien and other leaders are arrested and transported to Australia.

John O'Donovan publishes Volume One of his seven-volume translation of the *Annals of the Four Masters*.

1849

The potato crop fails again. The Irish countryside remains devastated by famine and there are further outbreaks of cholera.

Queen Victoria and Prince Albert visit Ireland.

Non-denominational Queen's Colleges in Belfast, Cork and Galway begin enrolling students.

The Dublin to Cork railway begins operating.

Dublin Zoo breeds the world's first lions in captivity.

The deaths of James Clarence Mangan (born 1803) from cholera and
Maria Edgeworth (born 1767), novelist.

1850

The Great Famine ends. Its aftermath of emigration and rural
deprivation lasts for over a century.

The Irish Tenant League is established.

The Representation Act increases the Irish electorate to 163,000.

The Queen's Colleges are chartered. The National Synod of Catholic
Bishops declares its opposition to Catholics attending.

1851

Census figures show that the population is now 6,575,000 – a drop of
1,600,000 in ten years.

Irish Members of Parliament form the Catholic Defence Association to
oppose new laws curtailing the rights of the Catholic hierarchy –
they are afterwards dubbed 'the Pope's Brass Band'.

A free medical care system is provided through plans to establish
dispensaries throughout Ireland.

Sheridan Le Fanu publishes *Ghost Stories and Tales of Mystery*.

1852

Vere Foster founds the Irish Female Emigration Fund. Scandal later
ensues when some of the girls it helps are found working in New
York brothels.

Craigmore Viaduct completed near Newry. It is one of the largest
engineering works of its era (designed by Sir John MacNeill).

The death of Thomas Moore (born 1779), the poet. His poems include
the 'The Last Rose of Summer' and many other works.

1853

Income Tax is introduced for the first time.

The vessel *Queen Victoria* sinks on rocks off Dublin Bay with the loss
of 55 lives. Deficiencies in the Baily Lighthouse contribute to the
disaster.

William Rowan Hamilton publishes his system of 'quarternion'
calculus.

Benjamin Lowe establishes one of the first Irish walking records when
he completes 500 miles in 500 hours for a wager.

1854

The Catholic University of Ireland opens in Dublin, with the
  prominent English Catholic, John Henry Newman, as its Rector.
The last Donnybrook Fair is held near Dublin.
Workmen constructing the Ennis Railway discover a hoard of over
  500 gold ornaments dating from about 500 BC.
Construction begins on the Museum Building, Trinity College
  (architect, Benjamin Woodward).
The Royal Hibernian Academy holds its first exhibition of Irish art.
 William Allingham publishes the second edition of *The Music Master*
  – with woodcuts by Ruskin and Millais.
John Mitchel publishes *Jail Journal* (New York).

1855

The first pillar post boxes in Ireland are erected in Dublin, Belfast and
  Ballymena.
The Emmet Monument Association is established in New York.
The Boyne Valley Viaduct, designed by Sir John MacNeill, is opened.
  The centre spans are replaced with a metal portion in 1932.

1856

Jeremiah O'Donovan Rossa forms the Phoenix Society in Skibbereen,
  Cork.
The University Church in Dublin, is consecrated (architect, J.H.
  Pollen).
William Carleton publishes *Willie Reilly and His Dear Colleen Bawn*.
The death of Father Theobald Mathew (born 1790).

1857

Rioting in Belfast follows the Twelfth of July celebrations – Loyalist
  marchers are blamed for provoking the violence.

1858

James Stephens founds the Irish Republican Brotherhood (IRB).
The transatlantic telegraph cable between Newfoundland and Valentia
  Island is completed.
The General Medical Council is founded in the UK. It includes Irish
  doctors.
The death of John Hogan (born 1800), sculptor.

1859

The Fenians, the Irish American equivalent of the IRB, are founded in
New York (their name becomes the popular description for Irish
revolutionaries up to about 1900).

George Adair purchases Glenveagh Estate, Co. Donegal (amongst the
largest private land purchases in Irish history).

The Catholic University of Ireland fails.

The Belleek Pottery opens a new factory building.

The Irish Times is founded by Major Laurence Knox.

1860

Deasy's Land Act increases the vulnerability of tenants.

The UK Parliament funds a scheme to replace farm labourers' cabins
with proper stone dwellings.

The Irish Volunteers of the 69th State Militia in New York refuse to
parade before the Prince of Wales.

The Archbishop of Dublin condemns mixed education.

Blackrock College, Co. Dublin, is opened by the Holy Ghost Fathers.

Dion Boucicault stages *The Colleen Bawn*.

1861

The census gives a population figure of 5,800,000, a decrease of over
11% since 1851.

The Glenveagh evictions follow the murder of George Adair's land
agent.

The American Civil War starts. Thomas Francis Meagher forms the
Irish Brigade from Irish immigrants in New York.

The deaths of the Gaelic scholar, John O'Donovan (born 1809), and
Benjamin Woodward, architect.

1862

Rainy weather and poor harvest cause hardship in the countryside.

The Poor Relief Act allows help for tenant farmers (excluded under
1847 Act).

The Irish Brigade fights heroically at the Battle of Antietam in the US
Civil War. Three months later at Fredericksburg it charges
Confederate Irish regiments on Mary's Heights.

The firm of Guinness adopts the trademark of a harp on a buff label.

The Harland and Wolff shipyard is founded in Belfast.

1863

James Stephens, with O'Donovan Rossa, Thomas Clarke Luby and John O'Leary, founds the Irish People.

The Irish Brigade suffers heavy casualties at the Battle of Gettysburg.

Thousands of Irish immigrants take part in the 'Conscription Riots' in New York.

Sheridan Le Fanu publishes *The House by the Church-Yard*.

1864

Work starts on the O'Connell Monument in Sackville Street, Dublin (sculptor, John Henry Foley). In Belfast, the burning of an effigy of O'Connell by Orangemen sparks off sectarian riots which result in at least a dozen deaths.

The National Gallery of Ireland opens.

Frederick Burton finishes the watercolour *The Meeting on the Turret Stairs*.

Sheridan Le Fanu publishes *Uncle Silas*.

The first Dublin Horse Show is held.

1865

Fenian leaders, including O'Donovan Rossa and Thomas Clarke Luby are imprisoned. James Stephens escapes.

Dublin newspapers now number 24.

Benjamin Lee Guinness begins restoration of St Patrick's Cathedral at his own expense.

William Lawrence opens a photographic studio in Dublin (the Lawrence Collection in the National Library numbers 40,000 plates – almost all taken after 1880 by Robert French).

Samuel Ferguson publishes *Lays of the Western Gael*. William Lecky publishes *History of the Rise and Fall of the Spirit of Rationalism in Europe*.

The death of Sir William Rowan Hamilton (born 1809), mathematician.

1866

Some 800 Fenians invade Canada from the United States – they occupy Fort Erie and fight a skirmish at Lime Ridgeway before withdrawing over the border.

Archbishop Cullen of Dublin is made a cardinal.

The death of George Petrie (born 1789), artist and antiquarian.
The first Irish Derby is staged at the Curragh.

1867

The Fenian rising in Ireland planned for March is betrayed and fails
  miserably. Thomas Kelly, leader of the Fenians, is arrested with his
  aide in Manchester. Fenians kill a policeman in an attempt to rescue
  Thomas Kelly (18 September). The 'Manchester Martyrs' – Allen,
  Larkin and O'Brien – are executed on 23 November. A Fenian bomb
  kills 14 in London (the Clerkenwell Explosion). In New York,
  Jerome J. Collins founds Clan na Gael.
Work commences on St Fin Barre's Protestant Cathedral, Cork.
William Lecky publishes *History of European Morals from Augustus
  to Charlemagne.*
The death of William Parsons Earl of Rosse (born 1800), astronomer.

1868

The Fenian bomber, Michael Barrett, is hanged in the last public
  execution in the British Isles.
The Irish Parliamentary Reform Act halves the borough qualification
  and gives lodgers the franchise.
The Irish National Teachers Association of Ireland is formed, with
  Vere Foster as its first president.
In Canada, the Minister of Agriculture, Thomas D'Arcy Magee, a poet
  and former Young Ireland patriot, is assassinated after condemning
  Fenian attacks.
The first horse-jumping competition at the Dublin Horse Show is held
  over two fences.
The death of Henry Cooke (born 1788), Presbyterian cleric.

1869

The Amnesty Association is formed after reports that Fenian prisoners
  are being persecuted in prison.
O'Donovan Rossa wins the Tipperary by-election in absentia
  (disqualified as a felon).
Isaac Butt forms a new Tenant League.
Charles Stewart Parnell is sent down from Cambridge University for
  rowdy behaviour.
The Irish Church Act dis-establishes the Church of Ireland.
The death of William Carleton (born 1794), writer.

1870

Isaac Butt founds the Home Rule Association to campaign for a
subordinate Irish Parliament.

Michael Davitt, leader of the IRB in England, is imprisoned.

Gladstone's first Land Act fails to improve the position of tenants.

The Belfast Telegraph is published for the first time.

P. W. Joyce publishes the final volume of *The Origin and History of
Irish Place Names*.

The deaths of Daniel Maclise (born 1806), artist, and Michael William
Balfe, composer.

1871

The census reveals that Ireland now has a population of 5,400,000.

O'Donovan Rossa and 32 other Fenian prisoners involved in the
Fenian raid on Canada are freed from prison.

The Gaiety Theatre opens in Dublin.

The Albert Memorial, London, is completed (the statue of Prince
Albert and the 'Asia' sculptural group by John Henry Foley, the
'Europe' sculptural group by Patrick MacDowell).

1872

Legislation provides for the secret ballot in Parliamentary elections.

There are sectarian riots in Belfast.

The Catholic Union is formed.

Trams begin running in Belfast and Dublin.

The penny-farthing bicycle first appears in Ireland.

Charles Lever publishes *Lord Kilgobbin.* Samuel Ferguson publishes
Congal.

1873

Isaac Butt founds the Home Rule League and the Confederation of
Great Britain in Manchester. Butt also founds the Home Rule League
in Dublin.

The Irish Universities Act is defeated by Irish Members of Parliament,
under pressure from the Catholic hierarchy, who object to its
provision for non-denominational education. Trinity College
abolishes its bar on Catholics enrolling.

Dromore Castle, Limerick, is completed.

Charles J. Kickham publishes *Knocknagow.*

1874

Fifty-five supporters of Home Rule win UK Parliamentary seats in the
  General Election. Isaac Butt's motion proposing Home Rule for
  Ireland is defeated in the House of Commons.

William Pirrie is taken into partnership by the Harland and Wolff
  shipyard.

Dion Boucicault stages *The Shagraun.*

J. P. Mahaffy publishes *Social Life in Greece from Homer to
  Menander*, noted for its frank treatment of homosexuality.

The Irish Football Union is formed (Dublin).

1875

Charles Stewart Parnell is elected to Parliament in the Meath by-
  election.

John Mitchel is elected to Parliament for Tipperary but is denied his
  seat because he is a convicted felon. Mitchel is re-elected for
  Tipperary but he dies before he can be unseated again.

The O'Connell Centenary year is marked with celebrations.

Catholic Bishops ban Catholics attending Trinity College and repeat
  their opposition to the Queen's Universities.

The Dublin Evening Chronicle closes after 156 years.

England beat Ireland in the inaugural Rugby International between the
  countries.

1876

The IRB splits with the Home Rule Party and demands that
  Fenian Members of Parliament withdraw from the House of
  Commons.

In America, Captain Miles Keogh and 31 Irish-born soldiers in the US
  Seventh Cavalry die at the Battle of the Little Big Horn (Custer
  massacre).

1877

A small group of Home Rule MPs led by Parnell obstruct the
  proceedings of the House of Commons.

Parnell takes over the leadership of the Home Rule Confederation
  from Isaac Butt.

Michael Davitt, a leading Fenian, is released from prison.

The Society for the Preservation of the Irish Language is founded (Dublin).

Percy French writes 'Abdallah Bulbul Ameer', his first famous song, for an amateur concert in Trinity College, Dublin.

1878

Michael Davitt proposes the 'New Departure' – linking land reform to the Nationalist Movement – in an article in *The New York Herald*.

The Earl of Leitrim and two companions are murdered in Donegal by land agitators.

A Board is established for secondary schools (Intermediate Education Act).

The Birr to Portumna line closes after only ten years – the shortest-lived Irish railway.

Bram Stoker enters a long-standing business partnership with Sir Henry Irvine, renowned English actor.

The death of William Stokes, medical scientist – the discoverer of Stokes-Adam's Syndrome and Cheyne-Stokes Respiration.

1879

Michael Davitt founds the Mayo Land League. At a meeting in Irishtown, the League initiates the 'Land War' to secure the 'Three Fs' (fair rent, fixity of tenure, free sale). Davitt forms the Irish National Land League with the support of C. S. Parnell.

An apparition of the Virgin appears at Knock, Co. Mayo.

Exceptionally heavy rains contribute to near famine conditions in many western areas.

Dan Lowry's Music Hall (today the Olympia Theatre) opens in Dublin.

The Irish Rugby Union is founded.

1880

Parnell tours America and addresses the US House of Representatives. Parnell is elected head of the Irish Parliamentary Party.

The Land League begins 'boycotting' its opponents (a practice named after Charles Boycott, Lord Erne's agent in Mayo).

In Dublin, the rebuilt Carlisle Bridge is renamed O'Connell Street Bridge.

Lord Ardilaun presents St Stephen's Green to the city of Dublin.

Tommy Beasley rides Empress (the first of his three Aintree Grand National winners) to victory in the 1880 Grand National (he wins on Woodbrook 1881, Frigate 1889).

1881

The census shows a population of under 5,200,000 – a decline of
3,000,000 since 1841.

Parnell is acquitted of criminal conspiracy charges.

Gladstone's Second Land Act grants the Three Fs. Parnell rejects the
Land Act over arrears issue and is imprisoned in Kilmainham Gaol.
The Land League is suppressed after issuing the 'No Rent
Manifesto'.

Dublin tram companies amalgamate into the Dublin United Tramway
Company.

The Dublin Horse Show is held at the Ballsbridge grounds for the first time.

The Royal Belfast Golf Club is established, the first in Ireland.

1882

In the 'Treaty of Kilmainham', Gladstone agrees to further reforms in
return for Parnell ending the Land War.

Chief Secretary Frederick Cavendish and Undersecretary Burke are
murdered in Phoenix Park by the 'Invincibles' (6 May).

The Irish National League is established to replace the suppressed
Land League.

A family of five are murdered in Co. Galway (the Maamtrasna murders).

The Tuke Committee is formed to give financial aid to emigrants – it
helps thousands to leave for America.

Oscar Wilde embarks on a lecture tour of the United States.

The death of Charles J. Kickham (born 1828).

1883

Five Invincibles are hanged for the Phoenix Park murders.

The Irish National League of America is founded.

The first electric tram in Ireland runs from Portrush to the Giant's
Causeway.

The Wilton Lawn Tennis Club is established.

1884

The Irish electorate increases by 350% when Gladstone extends the
vote to all householders.

The IRB commence a 'Dynamite Campaign'. Four Fenians are
sentenced to life imprisonment and three blow themselves up whilst
setting charges under London Bridge.

The National Maternity Hospital, Holles Street, is opened.

The first public libraries in Dublin (Capel Street and Thomas Street) are opened.

The Gaelic Athletic Association (GAA) is founded in Thurles, Tipperary. Archbishop Croke of Cashel becomes its patron.

Jack 'Nonpareil' Dempsey wins the first-ever middleweight world title boxing match at Great Kills, New York.

1885

Parnell makes his 'No man has the right to fix the boundaries to the march of a Nation' speech in Cork.

The Irish Party wins 85 seats in elections for the UK Parliament which gives them the balance of power.

Gladstone publicly gives his support to Home Rule (December).

The Irish Loyal and Patriotic Union is founded to defeat Home Rule.

The Orange Order calls on its lodges to demonstrate.

Fenians bomb the House of Commons, Tower of London, and Westminster Hall.

The 'Ashbourne' Act makes funds available to grant full loans for tenants wishing to buy their land.

Construction of the West Clare railway begins (opens 1887).

Work begins on the National Library and Science and Art Museum, Dublin.

The Irish Amateur Athletic Association is founded.

1886

Gladstone's Liberals are restored to power, after Irish Members of Parliament vote out Lord Salisbury's Conservative administration. Gladstone introduces the First Home Rule Bill in the House of Commons – it is defeated by 30 votes on its second reading and Parliament dissolves.

The Conservatives win the subsequent General Election, fought mainly on the Home Rule issue.

The Irish Unionist Party is founded to oppose Home Rule with the support of Joseph Chamberlain.

Lord Randolph Churchill makes the 'Ulster will fight; Ulster will be right' speech at the Ulster Hall, Belfast.

There is widespread sectarian rioting in Ulster – 31 people are killed in Belfast during July and August. Evictions are carried out for arrears of rent by the Marquis of Clanricard in Co. Galway. There are serious disturbances at Woodford and Portumna.

The Irish National Land League implements the 'Plan of Campaign' to fight landlords.

George Moore publishes *A Drama in Muslin*.

The death of Samuel Ferguson (born 1810), poet.

1887

The London Times publishes an alleged letter by Parnell condoning the Phoenix Park murders, and accuses him of complicity in the Land War violence.

Twenty-eight families are evicted in Bodyke, Co. Clare. Agitation for reform by the Plan of Campaign supporters culminates in the 'Mitchelstown Massacre' in Cork, when the RIC shoot dead three demonstrators.

Archbishop Croke denounces the GAA. as a Fenian organisation after an IRB candidate wins its presidency.

Lady Wilde publishes *Ancient Legends of Ireland*. Samuel Ferguson publishes *Oghm Inscriptions in Ireland, Wales and Scotland* posthumously.

The first All Ireland finals are staged by the GAA. In hurling, Thurles of Tipperary beat Meelick of Galway (1 April at Birr). In football, Commercials of Limerick beat Young Irelands of Dundalk (29 April at Clonskeagh).

1888

A Special Commission begins to investigate accusations made by *The London Times* against Parnell. The Catholic hierarchy condemn the Plan of Campaign. Parnell disassociates himself from the Land Movement . The Institute of Chartered Accountants of Ireland is founded. The Ballybunion to Listowel monorail line starts running.

Sir John Lavery is commissioned to paint Queen Victoria, which establishes him as a society portrait painter.

Oscar Wilde publishes *The Happy Prince*. P. W. Joyce publishes *Irish Music and Songs*. William Butler Yeats publishes *Folk and Fairy Tales of the Irish Peasantry*.

Ireland's first park racecourse is opened at Leopardstown, Co. Dublin.

There are no All Ireland Champions this year.

1889

Richard Pigott is exposed at the Special Commission as the author of the 'Parnell' letters; he shoots himself in Madrid a month later.

Parnell is vindicated and receives a standing ovation in the House of Commons. Captain W. H. O'Shea cites Parnell as co-respondent when he files for divorce from Kitty O'Shea.

Eighty people die in one of Ireland's worst ever train crashes at Armagh.

Horace Plunkett establishes the first co-operative creamery in Ireland at Drumcolliher, Limerick.

The Pioneer League is founded by Father James Cullen.

William Butler Yeats publishes *Wanderings of Oisin and Other Poems* and *Crossways*.

The All Ireland Champions are Dublin (hurling) and Tipperary (football).

The death of William Allingham (born 1824), poet. The long poem *Laurence Bloomfield in Ireland* is possibly his best known work.

1890

Captain O'Shea divorces his wife and wins custody of their children (17 November).

Parnell is re-elected as leader of Irish Parliamentary Party (25 November).

Gladstone states that Home Rule is impossible if Parnell remains as leader of the Irish Party.

Five leading Irish Members of Parliament oppose Parnell. The Irish Party meets in Committee Room 15 to debate his leadership. Some 44 Members of Parliament walk out of the meeting and withdraw from the party, leaving Parnell with only 28 followers (6 December).

A study finds that the most common Irish surnames are Murphy, Kelly, O'Sullivan and Walshe.

The Royal Society of Antiquaries of Ireland is founded.

Douglas Hyde publishes *Beside the Fire*.

The All Ireland Champions are Cork (hurling) and Cork (football).

The death of Dion Boucicault (born 1820), actor and playwright.

1891

The census shows a population 4,705,000.

The Balfour Act makes more funds available for land purchase and sets up the Congested Districts Board. Anti-Parnellites form the Irish National Federation and wins seats at Sligo North and Carlow.

Parnell marries Kitty O'Shea in Steyning, Sussex (June).

The death of Charles Stewart Parnell (born 1846) in Brighton (6 October) – 200,000 people attend his funeral in Dublin.

Michael Davitt, standing as an anti-Parnell candidate, is defeated by
  John Redmond in the Waterford city by-election.
James Stephens, founder of the IRB, returns home after 25 years in exile.
The *Irish Daily Independent* newspaper (from 1905 *Irish Independent*)
  is founded.
Oscar Wilde publishes *The Picture of Dorian Gray*.
The All Ireland Champions are Kerry (hurling) and Dublin (football).

1892

The Belfast Labour Party (the first Socialist party in Ireland) is
  established in Belfast.
Free primary schooling and compulsory education up to the age of 14
  is introduced through the Irish Education Act.
Professor John Joly, of Trinity College, Dublin, invents the first
  practical colour photographic process.
The Irish National Literary Society is founded.
Oscar Wilde stages *Lady Windemere's Fan*.
The first Irish Golf Championship is held.
The All Ireland Champions are Cork (hurling) and Dublin (football).

1893

Gladstone's Second Home Rule Bill is defeated in the House of Lords.
Opposition to Home Rule by Northern Protestants manifests in mass
  demonstrations in Belfast (4 April).
Douglas Hyde and Eoin Mac Néill found the Gaelic League.
Consecration of St Mel's Cathedral, Longford, which took 53 years to
  build.
Douglas Hyde publishes *Love Songs of Connacht*. William Butler
  Yeats publishes *The Rose*. Oscar Wilde stages *A Woman of No
  Importance*.
The All Ireland Champions are Cork (hurling) and Wexford (football).

1894

Gladstone retires from politics.
The first meeting of the Irish Trade Union Congress.
The Irish Agricultural Organisation Society is established under
  Horace Plunkett to encourage the Co-operative Movement.
In the Bridget Cleary murder case in Tipperary, Bridget was killed by
  her husband because he believed she was a fairy changeling.

Somerville and Ross publish *The Real Charlotte*. George Moore
  publishes *Esther Waters*.
The All Ireland Champions are Cork (hurling) and Dublin (football).

1895

Michael Davitt enters the House of Commons as the Member of
  Parliament for South Mayo. He was refused entry on two previous
  occasions because of felony rule.
Oscar Wilde collapses under cross-examination by Edward Carson in
  his libel case against Lord Queensberry; later in the year he is
  imprisoned for two years on homosexuality charges.
Oscar Wilde stages *An Ideal Husband* and *The Importance of Being
  Earnest*.
The All Ireland Champions are Tipperary (hurling) and Tipperary
  (football).

1896

James Connolly founds the Irish Republican Socialist Party.
John Dillon assumes the leadership of the anti-Parnellite wing of the
  Home Rule Party.
An extension to Balfour's Land Act makes 1,500 bankrupt estates
  available for sale to tenants.
Ireland's first motor vehicle laws are introduced.
The first electric tram runs in Dublin.
The Limavady hoard of prehistoric gold objects is discovered by Tom
  Nicholl whilst ploughing.
Ireland's first cinema shows are held at Dan Lowry's Music Hall,
  Dublin.
John Pius Boland wins gold medals for tennis (singles and doubles) at
  the first modern Olympic Games in Athens.
The All Ireland Champions are Tipperary (hurling) and Limerick
  (football).
The death of Lady Wilde (Speranza), writer and mother of Oscar
  Wilde.

1897

The Irish Motor Car and Cycle Company begins operating.
Bram Stoker publishes *Dracula*. Amanda McKittrick Ros publishes
  Irene Iddesleigh.
The All Ireland Champions are Limerick (hurling) and Dublin (football).

1898

The Local Government (Ireland) Act establishes popularly elected local authorities and gives qualified women a vote for the first time.

James Connolly launches the weekly *Workers' Republic*.

The Mary Immaculate College, Limerick, is founded to train women Catholic national school teachers.

Dr John Colohan of Blackrock, Co. Dublin, imports the first petrol driven motor car (a Benz) into Ireland.

The Gaelic League holds its first féis at Macroom, Cork.

Oscar Wilde publishes *The Ballad of Reading Gaol.*

The All Ireland Champions are Tipperary (hurling) and Dublin (football).

1899

The Boer War starts in South Africa. Major John McBride forms an Irish Brigade to aid the Boers. Michael Davitt withdraws from the House of Commons in protest at the Boer War.

The first issue of Arthur Griffith's journal, *United Irishman.*

W.B. Yeats and Edward Martin form the Irish Literary Theatre (first prduction Yeats's *The Countess Cathleen*).

The Rathmines and Rathgar Music Society founded.

Somerville and Ross publish *Experiences of an Irish RM*. William Butler Yeats publishes *The Wind Amongst the Reeds.*

Tom Kiely establishes a world record in the hammer event and becomes the first man to throw the hammer more than 160 feet (49 metres).

The All Ireland Champions are Tipperary (hurling) and Dublin (football).

1900

The Parnellite and anti-Parnellite factions of the Home Rule Party reunite under the leadership of John Redmond.

Arthur Griffith founds Cumann na nGaedheal.

The Irish Guards regiment of the British army is established.

The earliest surviving film is made in Ireland (of Queen Victoria's visit to Dublin).

The All Ireland Champions are Tipperary (hurling) and Tipperary (football).

Oscar Wilde (born 1854) dies in Paris.

1901

The census shows the population is 4,459,000.

The Irish Literary Theatre stages the first professional performance of a play in the Irish language (*Borny Douglas Hyde*).

The All Ireland Champions are London (hurling)and Dublin (football).

The death of Vere Foster (born 1819), educationalist.

1902

The UK Liberal Party abandons its support for Home Rule.

The Dunraven Land Conference is held between tenants and landlords.

W. B. Yeats stages *Cathleen ní Houlihan*. George Russell stages *Deirdre*. Lady Gregory publishes *Cuchulainn of Muirthemne*.

The All Ireland Champions are Cork (hurling) and Dublin (football).

1903

Wyndham's Land Act helps tenants to buy out leases.

St Patrick's Day is made an official holiday.

The Independent Orange Order is founded in Belfast.

The Irish Literary Theatre becomes the Irish National Theatre.

The An Túr Gloine (the Glass Tower) stained glass studio is set up in Dublin.

The first Gordon Bennet Race for automobiles is held over a course in Laois, Offaly and Kildare.

The All Ireland Champions are Cork (hurling) and Kerry (football).

The death of Ellen Blackburn, suffragette.

1904

The Irish Reform Association is formed by Lord Dunraven to campaign for devolution.

Rioters drive out Limerick's Jewish population (the Limerick Pogrom).

Robert and Jack Chambers begin to manufacture Chambers automobiles in Belfast. They produce 16 different models over the next 21 years.

Work begins on the Government Buildings, Dublin (architects, Webb and Deanne).

The Abbey Theatre opens in Dublin with plays by W. B. Yeats and Lady Gregory.

Bloomsday (June 10) – James Joyce meets Nora Barnacle in Dublin and later sets his novel *Ulysses* on this day.

W. B. Yeats refuses to stage Shaw's *John Bull's Other Island* at the Abbey Theatre. J. M. Synge stages *Riders to the Sea*.

Lady Gregory publishes *Gods and Fighting Men*.

The All Ireland Champions are Kilkenny (hurling) and Kerry (football).

1905

Arthur Griffith proposes the Sinn Féin (We Ourselves) policy.

The first of the Dungannon Clubs is formed in Belfast by Nationalists.

The Ulster Unionist Council is founded. It helps forge links between Unionists and the Orange Order.

The Independent Orange Order issue the Magheramore Manifesto.

Electric trams begin running in Belfast.

George Bernard Shaw stages *Major Barbara* and *Man and Superman*.

George Moore publishes *The Lake*.

De Profundis by Oscar Wilde is published posthumously.

The All Ireland Champions are Kilkenny (hurling) and Kildare (football).

1906

A cross-channel boat service begins from Rosslare Harbour, near Wexford.

The Belfast City Hall is completed (architect, Alfred Blumwell Thomas).

The first issue of *Sinn Féin*.

John McCormack makes his stage debut in Savona, Italy.

The All Ireland Champions are Tipperary (hurling) and Dublin (football).

The death of Michael Davitt (born 1846).

1907

Cumann na nGaedheal and the Dungannon Clubs become the Sinn Féin League (21 April). The National Council merges with the Sinn Féin League (5 September) and in September 1908 it adopts the name Sinn Féin.

The Evicted Tenants Act reinstates tenants and gives statutory purchase rights to the Land Commission on their behalf.

James Larkin organises the Belfast Docks Strike, which lasts from May to September.

Pope Pius X issues the Ne Temere Decree. It states that mixed marriages are only valid if the wedding service is held in Catholic churches and children from the union must be raised in the Catholic faith.

Marconi begins his transatlantic wireless service between Clifden and Canada.

There are riots in Dublin (Abbey Riots) after John Synge's *Playboy of the Western World* is first staged.

Padraic Colum publishes *Wild Earth*. J. M. Synge publishes *The Aran Islands*.

The All Ireland Champions are Kilkenny (hurling) and Dublin (football).

1908

The Irish Universities Act restructures the Royal University into the National University of Ireland (with colleges in Dublin, Galway and Cork) and Queen's University, Belfast.

Patrick Pearse opens St Enda's School for Boys, Rathmines.

The Government sets up a fund to help local authorities house poorer classes. The The Old Age Pension is introduced.

The Dublin Municipal Gallery is opened through the efforts of Hugh Lane.

The All Ireland Champions are Tipperary (hurling) and Dublin (football).

1909

Fianna Éireann is formed under the leadership of Countess Marcievicz.

James Larkin forms the Irish Transport and General Workers Union (ITGWU).

Birrell's Land Act gives the congested Districts Board the right to compulsorily purchase land for the rationalisation of holdings.

The first flight by an Irish plane is made by Harry Ferguson at Hillsborough.

The Volta Cinema, Ireland's first cinema, opens in Dublin under the management of James Joyce.

George Bernard Shaw's *The Shewing up of Blanco Posnet* is staged in Dublin after it is banned in London.

Joseph Campbell publishes *The Mountainy Singer*.

The All Ireland Champions are Kilkenny (hurling)and Kerry (football).

The death of John Millington Synge (born 1871).

1910

Sir Edward Carson is elected leader of the Unionist Party.

First issue of *Irish Freedom*, IRB monthly newspaper.

Irish is made compulsory for entry to the National University of
  Ireland.

The White Star Liner *Olympic* is launched at the Harland and Wolff
  shipyard, Belfast.

Sidney Olcott begins making films in Ireland with the US Kalem
  Company – the first film is *The Lad from Ould Ireland*.

James Connolly publishes *Labour in Irish History*.

The All Ireland Champions are Wexford (hurling) and Louth
  (football).

1911

The census of Ireland shows the population as 4,400,000 – almost
  halved since 1841.

The Dublin Employers' Federation is established to oppose organised labour.

The Irish Women Workers Union is formed. Qualified women win the
  right to membership of local councils and boroughs.

The *Titanic*, sister ship of the *Olympic*, is launched at Harland and
  Wolff.

James Larkin publishes *The Irish Worker*, the newspaper of the
  ITGWU.

The Parnell Monument in Sackville Street, Dublin, is inaugurated
  (sculptor, Augustus Saint Gaudens). The Cuchulainn Statue, now in the
  GPO building, is designed by Oliver Sheppard.

The All Ireland Champions are Kilkenny (hurling) and Cork
  (football).

1912

Asquith introduces the Third Home Rule Bill. A Unionist amendment
  tries to keep Ulster in the United Kingdom but it is defeated. On
  'Ulster Day', almost 500,000 Ulster men and women sign the
  Solemn League and Covenant in protest against Home Rule.

The Irish Labour Party is founded at the Irish Trade Union Congress
  in Clonmel, Tiperary.

Father Browne, an Irish priest, takes photographs aboard the *Titanic* at
  sea. The *Titanic* hits an iceberg and sinks on her maiden voyage –
  some 1,490 people are drowned and 711 saved (14 and 15 April).

D. W. Corbett makes the first aeroplane crossing of the Irish Sea.

James Stephens publishes *The Crock of Gold.*

The All Ireland Champions are Kilkenny (hurling) and Cork (football).

The death of Bram Stoker (born 1847).

1913

The Third Home Rule Bill is carried in the House of Commons but defeated in the House of Lords twice (January and July).

The Ulster Volunteer Force (UVF) is formed in Belfast.

The Unionist Council sets up a 'Provisional Government' under the leadership of Edward Carson.

The League for the Support of Ulster is established in Britain.

The Dublin Lock-out takes place from 26 August to early February 1914. William Martin Murphy fires 40 members of the ITGWU (18 August). James Larkin responds with a general strike. There is then an Employers Federation lock-out of employees (26 August), followed by rioting in Dublin. James Connolly and James Larkin are imprisoned for short terms (August–September). The locked-out workers and their families suffer great hardship. The British Trade Union Movement sends food ships to Dublin (27 September, 4 October).

A Citizen army is raised from Dublin workers. The Irish Volunteers are founded.

Francis O'Neill, a Chicago policeman, publishes *Irish Minstrels and Musicians.* Joseph Campbell publishes *Irishry.*

The All Ireland Champions are Kilkenny (hurling) and Kerry (football).

1914

The Curragh Mutiny – 57 officers of the British army declare they will refuse to implement Home Rule. The authorities take no disciplinary action.

The UVF land a large shipment of arms from the vessel *Clydevalley* at Larne and Bangor.

The Provisional Government of Ulster meets for the first time.

The Home Rule Bill passes the House of Commons for the third time but is stalled in the House of Lords over the Ulster question (8 July).

Erskine Childers brings arms into Howth on the *Asgard.* British troops kill4 and wound 27 on Bachelor's Walk.

Britain declares war on Germany (4 August). The Home Rule Bill is suspended until hostilities cease.

The Woodenbridge Speech – John Redmond calls on the Irish
  Volunteers to serve with the British Armed Forces (20 September).
  The Volunteers split into the moderate National Volunteers and the
  militant Irish Volunteers.

The Report into the Housing of the Dublin Working Classes reveals
  that almost 90,000 people are living in sub-standard accommodation.
  'Darkest Dublin' – a collection of photographs of the slums of
  Dublin – is published.

James Joyce publishes *Dubliners*.

The All Ireland Champions are Kilkenny (hurling) and Kerry
  (football).

1915

The Military Council of the IRB is set up. Its leaders include Patrick
  Pearse, Eamon Ceannt and Joseph Plunkett, later joined by Thomas
  J. Clarke and Seán MacDiarmada.

Militant Nationalists take control of the Gaelic League – Douglas
  Hyde is replaced as President by Eoin MacNéill.

The *Lusitania* is sunk by a German submarine off the Cork coast. Sir
  Hugh Lane is among the 1,198 dead.

The Dublin Fusiliers and Munster Fusiliers suffer heavy casualties in
  the Gallipoli landings, losing 600 and 550 men respectively (April).

Francis Ledwidge publishes *Songs of the Earth*.

The deaths of Viola Martin or 'Ross' (born1862), writer, and Jeremiah
  O'Donovan Rossa (born1831). Patrick Pearse gives O'Donovan
  Rossa's funeral oration in Dublin (1 August).

The All Ireland Champions are Laois (hurling) and Wexford (football).

1916

James Connolly joins the Military Council of the IRB – a rising is
  planned for 23 April, Easter Sunday.

The *Aud*, with 20,000 rifles and munitions sails from Germany (9
  April). A submarine follows with Roger Casement (12 April). The
  Aud is arrested in Tralee Bay by a British naval patrol (20 April),
  then scuttled by her crew in Cork Harbour (21 April). Roger
  Casement lands with two companions at Banna Strand, Fenit, near
  Tralee. He is arrested by British forces within a few hours (21 April).

Eoin MacNéill places a newspaper advertisement cancelling Volunteer
  'manouevres' on Easter Sunday. The IRB Military Council reverse
  the order (23 April).

The Easter Rising begins; the GPO is occupied by Volunteers and
Patrick Pearse reads the Proclamation of the Irish Republic from its
steps. Boland's Mills, the College of Surgeons and other Dublin
buildings are seized by the rebels (24 April). General Lowe declares
Martial Law and moves British reinforcements into the centre of
Dublin. The Citizen army garrison in the College of Surgeons is
overwhelmed (26 April). British troops secure the Liffey quays and
isolate the GPO. A navy gunboat bombards the city centre. The
Sherwood Foresters are ambushed at the Mount Street Bridge by
Volunteers – they suffer over 230 casualties (26 April). Francis
Sheehy-Skeffington (born 1878) and two others are murdered by
Captain J. C. Bowen-Colthurst. An IRB force under Thomas Ashe
attacks the RIC at Ashbourne Meath (27 April). Patrick Pearse
surrenders to General Lowe at the GPO (29 April). The Easter
Rising casualties (dead and wounded) include 184 insurgents, 530
British Forces and 2,300 civilians. Captured insurgents, including
Eamon de Valera, Michael Collins and Countess Marcievicz, are sent
to be interned in England.

The following insurgent leaders are executed at Kilmainham Gaol in
Dublin: on 3 May, Patrick Pearse (born 1879), Thomas Clarke (born
1857), Thomas MacDonagh (born 1878); on 4 May, Edward Daly,
Michael O'Hanrahan, William Pearse, Thomas Plunkett (born 1887,
he marries Francis Gifford a few hours before his execution); on 5
May, John MacBride (born 1865); on 8 May, Eamon Ceannt (born
1881), Con Colbert, Seán Heuston and Michael Mallin; on 12 May,
James Connolly (born 1868) and Seán MacDiarmada (born 1884).

Thomas Kent is executed in Cork on 9 May.

Roger Casement is tried in England and sentenced to death (29 June).
The 'Black Journal' (possibly forged by British intelligence) is
circulated to discourage a reprieve. Casement (born 1864) is hanged
at Pentonville Prison on 3 August.

Lloyd George seeks to negotiate a Home Rule agreement which
excludes six Ulster counties. This is rejected by John Redmond (of
the Irish Parliamentary Party). The first of the Easter Rising
internees in England are freed and return home (December).

At the Battle of the Somme in France (1–11 July), the 36th (Ulster)
Division suffer over 5,000 casualties.

The Twelfth of July Orange Marches are cancelled and replaced with a
five-minute silence.

The 16th (Irish) Division suffers 4,500 casualties at Ginchy in the later stages of the Somme offensive (September).

Lennox Robinson stages *The Whiteheaded Boy*.

James Joyce publishes *Portrait of the Artist as a Young Man*. James Stephens publishes *Insurrection in Dublin*.

The All Ireland Champions are Tipperary (hurling) and Wexford (football).

1917

The remaining Easter Rising internees are released from prison (June).

Eamon de Valera wins the Clare East by-election (July 10). Other Sinn Féin candidates win by-elections in Roscommon North (February), Longford South (May) and Kilkenny City (August). Lloyd George convenes the Irish Convention but Sinn Féin refuse to participate (25 July–1 August 1918). The Sinn Féin Ard Féis is held at the Mansion House, Dublin; Eamon de Valera is elected President (25 October). The Irish Volunteers elect de Valera as their leader (26 October).

At the Battle of Messines Ridge, Flanders, the 16th (Irish) Division fights alongside the 36th (Ulster) Division.

The All Ireland Champions are Dublin (hurling) and Wexford (football).

Thomas Ashe (born 1885) dies as the result of a hunger strike in Mountjoy Gaol and Francis Ledwidge (born 1887) is killed in the second Battle of Ypres.

1918

Voting rights are extended to all men over 21 and qualified women over 30.

The Military Service Act introduces conscription but it is abandoned when opposed by the Church, the Home Rule Party and Sinn Féin. Eamon de Valera and leading Nationalists are interned over the non-existent 'German Plot' (May).

Five hundred are drowned when the *Kingstown*, a Holyhead mailboat, sinks.

World War I ends (11 November) – some 350,000 Irishmen served with the British army during its course, of whom at least 35,000 were killed.

There is a General Election in the UK. The Home Rule Party wins only 6 seats. Sinn Féin candidates, who state they will boycott Parliament, win 73 seats. Unionist candidates win 26 seats. Countess

Marcievicz, of Sinn Féin, is the first woman to win a seat in the House of Commons (December).

Brinsley MacNamara publishes *Valley of the Squinting Windows*.

The All Ireland Champions are Limerick (hurling) and Wexford (football).

The death of John Redmond (born 1856).

1919

Sinn Féin convenes the first Dáil Éireann (Irish Parliament), which issues a Declaration of Independence and elects Cathal Brugha as Acting President (21/22 January).

The War of Independence begins at Soloheadbeag, Co. Tipperary, when two RIC men are killed by Volunteers (21 January). Eamon de Valera escapes from Lincoln Jail (February). The Dáil Éireann elects Eamon de Valera as President (1 April). Sinn Féin is suppressed, first in Tipperary then in other disturbed areas.

There are widespread ambushes, arms raids and assassinations. British soldiers loot shops and homes in Fermoy and Cork City. The 'Limerick Soviet' seizes control of the city after local unions call a general strike (April).

Alcock and Brown land in Clifden, Galway, after completing the first non-stop transatlantic flight.

W. B. Yeats publishes *The Wild Swans at Coole*.

The All Ireland Champions are Cork (hurling) and Kildare (football).

1920

'Black and Tan' police units (composed of former British army soldiers recruited in England) arrive in Ireland to reinforce the RIC.

Tomás MacCurtain, Mayor of Cork, is assassinated in his home by the RIC.

The Irish Republican Army (IRA) is established and attacks police barracks throughout Ireland. Crown forces attack civilian property in Limerick, Mallow, Trim, Cork and other centres.

The Black and Tans sack the small town of Balbriggan, near Dublin (20 September).

Terence MacSwiney, Mayor of Cork, dies while on a hunger strike in Brixton Prison (25 October).

Kevin Barry, aged 18, becomes the youngest IRA man executed in the War (1 November).

The Michael Collins' 'Squad' kill 14 British intelligence officers at
locations throughout Dublin (night of 20 November). The Black and
Tans open fire at Croke Park on the following day, killing 14
spectators and a player ('Bloody Sunday'). The UK Parliament
passes the so-called 'partition act' (the Act for the Better
Government of Ireland).

There is sectarian rioting in Derry (19 killed) and Belfast (13 killed).
Hundreds of Catholic families living in Protestant areas flee during
July and August.

The Royal Ulster Constabulary and Ulster Special Constabulary are
established.

Irish soldiers of the Connaught Rangers mutiny in India – one man is
executed and others receive long prison sentences.

The All Ireland Champions are Dublin (hurling) and Tipperary
(football).

The death of Percy French (born 1854), composer of the song, 'The
Mountains of Mourne'.

1921

Sir James Craig replaces Edward Carson as leader of the Unionist
Party.

The first elections are held for the new Northern Ireland Parliament.

The Northern Ireland Parliament is formally opened by George V (22
June). The Southern Parliament is boycotted by Sinn Féin and
adjourns (28 June).

Custom House, Dublin, is burnt down by the IRA. A truce between
Sinn Féin and the British Government comes into operation (11
July). Anti-Catholic riots in Belfast in response to the truce claim 16
lives (July). Sinn Féin convenes the Second Dáil Éireann (16
August) and sends a delegation led by Michael Collins and Arthur
Griffith to London (9 October).

At the Anglo–Irish Conference, Lloyd George insists that the six
Ulster counties remain outside of an independent Ireland. He
threatens to resume hostilities within three days (11 October–6
December). The Anglo-Irish Treaty is signed by the Irish delegation,
excluding the six Ulster counties (6 December). De Valera rejects the
Treaty (8 December).

Proportional representation replaces the majority vote in Local
Government elections.

The All Ireland Champions are Limerick (hurling) and Dublin (football).

1922

The Dáil Éireann ratifies the Anglo–Irish Treaty by 64–57 votes (7 January). De Valera resigns as the President of Sinn Féin and leads the anti-Treaty faction out of the Dáil (9/10 January).

Arthur Griffith is elected President of Dáil Éireann, and Michael Collins is appointed Chairman of the Provisional Government. Dublin Castle is handed over to Michael Collins and British rule in Ireland ends (16 January). The 'League of the Republic' is formed by Eamon de Valera. Anti-Treaty IRA members form their own Army Council under Liam Lynch. The Four Courts, Dublin, are occupied by the anti-Treaty IRA (14 April).The first Irish Free State General Election is held – the pro-Treaty candidates win a clear majority (16 June). The IRA Convention splits on the issue of the Treaty (18 June).

The Irish Civil War begins. The Free State forces shell the Four Courts (28 June).

The Free State Government captures the Four Courts (30 June) and gains control of Dublin. The Free State Army captures Waterford and Limerick (July), Cork city (10 August) and Fermoy (11 October). The Dáil gives Military Courts the right to sentence prisoners to death (October). Seventy-seven anti-Treaty Republicans are executed during the course of the war.

During sectarian riots in Ulster in June and July over 450 people are killed in Belfast alone. Thousands of Catholics flee Ulster. The IRA assassinate Sir Henry Wilson (born 1864) in London.

Michael Collins (born 1890) is killed in an ambush at Béal na mBláth, Co. Cork (22 August).

The Dáil elects William Thomas Cosgrave as head of its Provisional Government (9 September).

The All Ireland Champions are Kilkenny (hurling) and Dublin (football).

The UK Parliament Act establishes the Irish Free State (6 December).

Arthur Griffith (born 1871) and Erskine Childers (born 1870) are executed by the Free State.

1923

De Valera orders anti-Treaty forces to cease fighting (27 April). The Civil War ends (24 May).

W. T. Cosgrave establishes the Cumann na nGaedheal Party.

In the Free State General Election, W. T. Cosgrave retains power (Eamon de Valera and 43 other Sinn Féin members of the new Dáil abstain). The Irish Free State joins the League of Nations.

The Garda Síochána are established.

The Free State abolishes workhouses.

The Land Commission takes over the duties of the Congested Districts Board.

An Irish Film Censor is appointed. The Appeals Board includes W. B. Yeats.

The United Council of Christian Churches and Communions is formed, representing Methodists, Presbyterians and the Church of Ireland.

W. B. Yeats wins the Nobel Prize for Literature.

Seán O'Casey stages *Shadow of a Gunman*. George Bernard Shaw stages *St Joan*.

Daniel Corkery publishes *The Hidden Ireland*.

James Joyce publishes *Ulysses*.

The All Ireland Champions are Galway (hurling) and Dublin (football).

The death of Edward Martyn (born 1859), co-founder of the Abbey Theatre.

1924

The Boundary Commission meets in London. In the 'Army Mutiny', two Government ministers resign after officers object to a reduction of the army by 25,000 soldiers; General Eoin O'Duffy is appointed the new commander-in-chief.

The Free State Air Corps is founded.

The Intermediate and Leaving Certificate Examinations are established.

The first regular air service between Ireland and Britain is inaugurated (Belfast to Liverpool).

The Film Censor bans 104 films.

The All Ireland Champions are Dublin (hurling) and Kerry (football).

1925

Boundary Commission findings are leaked by *The Morning Post*. The two Governments agree to retain the existing Ulster/Free State border.

In the Northern Ireland General Election, the Unionists gain almost total control of the Northern Ireland Parliament.

The IRA breaks with Eamon de Valera and forms an independent Army Council.

Legislation allowing divorce is effectively barred in the Free State.

Annual examinations for entrance into the Irish Civil Service are introduced.

Construction work on the Shannon Hydro-electric Scheme begins.

Production starts on the Thomond Car – believed to be the first automobile manufactured in the Irish Free State.

The film *Irish Destiny* is released.

Seán O'Casey stages *Juno and the Paycock*.

Liam O'Flaherty publishes *The Informer*.

The All Ireland Champions are Tipperary (hurling) and Galway (football).

1926

The Irish Free State Census: 2,972,000. The Northern Ireland Census: 1,257,000.

Eamon de Valera breaks with Sinn Féin and founds the Fianna Fáil Party (May16).

The 2RN radio station is established in Dublin.

The staging of Seán O'Casey's *The Plough and The Stars* at the Abbey Theatre leads to rioting.

George Bernard Shaw is awarded the Nobel Prize for Literature.

The first Aga Khan Trophy Competition (for military teams) is held at the Dublin Horse Show.

The All Ireland Champions are Cork (hurling) and Kerry (football).

1927

In the Free State General Election, Cumann na nGaedheal retain power but are forced to resign when Eamon de Valera and 42 other abstaining Fianna Fáil members re-enter the Dáil (August). Cumann na nGaedheal narrowly defeat Fianna Fail in a second General Election (September).

Compulsory school attendance up to the age of 14 is introduced.

The Electricity Supply Board (ESB) is established under Thomas McLaughlin, architect of the Shannon Scheme. The Agricultural Credit Corporation is founded.

Kevin O'Higgins, Minister for Justice, is assassinated by Republican
    gunmen.
Henry Seagrave sets a new world land speed record at Daytona Beach,
    Florida.
The All Ireland Champions are Dublin (hurling) and Kildare
    (football).
The deaths of Countess Marcievicz (born 1868) and John Dillon (born
    1851), the Home Rule politician.

1928

New Irish coinage is issued, featuring the harp on one side and Irish
    animals and birds on the other (designer, Percy Metcalfe).
Irish is declared a compulsory subject for the Intermediate
    Certificate.
The Bremen makes the first east–west transatlantic air crossing – from
    Baldonnell Airport to Greely Island, Labrador.
The last sighting of a golden eagle in Ireland (Donegal).
Micheal Mac Liammóir and Hilton Edwards establish the Gate
    Theatre Company.
John McCormack is appointed a Papal count for his services to music.
W. B. Yeats publishes *The Tower*. Peadar O'Donnell publishes
    Islanders.
The first Irish team attends the Olympic Games. Pat O'Callaghan wins
    a gold medal in the hammer throwing event.
The All Ireland Champions are Cork (hurling) and Kildare
    (football).

1929

Northern Ireland abolishes proportional representation.
The first Irish banknotes are issued.
The Censorship of Publications Act establishes the Irish Censorship
    Board.
The Centenary of Catholic Emancipation celebrations are held.
Ardnacrusha Power Station opened on the Shannon Scheme.
Alfred Hitchcock films *Juno and the Paycock* with the Abbey Theatre
    cast (in London).
Elizabeth Bowen publishes *Last September*.
The All Ireland Champions are Cork (hurling) and Kerry
    (football).

1930

The Labour Party separates from Irish Trade Union Congress.

The Censorship Board begins banning books and publications.

The Dublin Corporation area expanded to include new suburbs.

The first Irish Sweepstakes draw.

Micheál MacLiammóir opens the Gate Theatre in Dublin.

Henry Seagrave (born 1896) is killed whilst setting a new world Water speed record on Lake Windermere, England.

The All Ireland Champions are Tipperary (hurling) and Kerry (football).

1931

W. T. Cosgrave secures the Statute of Westminster from Britain, giving Dominions the right to repeal or amend UK acts which are part of their law.

Seán Mac Bride founds Saor Éire.

The Free State Public Safety Act extends police powers and sets up a Military Tribunal to try political crimes – 12 organisations are banned, including the IRA and Saor Éire.

The An Óige Youth Hostel Movement is founded.

Building work starts on the Church of Christ the King, Cork (architects, B. Byrne and J. R. Boyd-Barrett).

Eamon de Valera founds *The Irish Press* newspaper.

Frank O'Connor publishes *Guests of the Nation*.

The All Ireland Champions are Cork (hurling) and Kerry (football).

The death of William Orpen (born 1878), artist.

1932

After the Irish Free State General Election, Eamon de Valera forms a Fianna Fáil Government.

The Free State Government suspends its Military Tribunal and releases political prisoners.

The Parliamentary Oath of Allegiance is abolished by De Valera.

A 'Trade War' begins over De Valera's cancellation of annuity payments due to Britain for loans made in the Land Reform era. Britain retaliates by imposing heavy customs duties on imported Irish goods.

The Army Comrades Association is founded from ex-soldiers of the Free State Army.

Eamon de Valera is inaugurated as Chairman of the League of Nations.

The Northern Ireland Parliament moves to a new building at Stormont,
   which is officially opened by Edward, Prince of Wales.
Unemployed Catholic and Protestant workers riot in Belfast.
The Eucharistic Congress is held in Dublin. It also commemorates
   1,500 years of Irish Christianity.
Maurice Walshe publishes *Blackcock's Feather*.
The All Ireland Champions are Kilkenny (hurling) and Kerry
   (football).

1933

Fianna Fáil retain power in the Irish Free State General Election.
The Army Comrade's Association elects Eoin O'Duffy as President. It
   changes its name to the National Guard and members receive the
   nickname 'Blueshirts'. The National Guard is proclaimed as an
   illegal organisation (August). The National Guard merges with
   Cumann na nGaedheal and the National Centre Party to form the
   United Ireland Party (later Fine Gael) under the leadership of
   O'Duffy (2 September). The Communist Party of Ireland is re-
   founded.
The All Ireland Champions are Kilkenny (hurling) and Cavan
   (football).

1934

Eoin O'Duffy resigns from the Fine Gael Party.
Pensions are given to the anti-Treaty Civil War veterans.
The Free State and UK Governments sign a Coal-Cattle agreement.
Changes in the primary school syllabus place greater emphasis on the
   Irish language and nationalist attitudes.
Irish is declared a compulsory subject for the Leaving Certificate.
Robert Flaherty's documentary film *Man of Aran* is premiered.
The All Ireland Champions are Limerick (hurling) and Galway
   (football).

1935

W. T. Cosgrave is elected chairman of Fine Gael.
There is rioting in Belfast (May).
The importation and sale of contraceptives is banned.
The All Ireland Champions are Kilkenny (hurling)and Cavan (football).
The death of George William Russell (born 1867), the writer and artist
   known as AE.

1936

The Irish Free State Census: 2,969,000.

The Free State Government severs most of the remaining links with Britain in preparation for the introduction of a new constitution. The Senate of the Irish Free State is abolished.

The IRA is declared an illegal organisation. The annual commemoration at Wolfe Tone's grave in Bodenstown is banned. Fine Gael expels the Blueshirts. Henry Boyle Somerville, retired British admiral, is assassinated by the IRA.

The Spanish Civil War begins. General Eoin O'Duffy leads 450 Blueshirts to join Franco's forces.

Frank Ryan and other Republican sympathisers make their way separately to Spain, where they form the 150-strong James Connolly Column of the International Brigade.

Irish Sea Airways – later Aer Lingus, the national airline – opens its first route, from Baldonnell Airport to Bristol using a DH 84.

The Dawn is made in Killarney – the first Irish feature film with sound.

Oliver St John Gogarty publishes *As I Was Going Down Sackville Street*. Seán O'Faolain publishes *Bird Alone*.

The All Ireland Champions are Limerick (hurling) and Mayo (football).

1937

Northern Ireland Census: 1,280,000.

Eamon de Valera's new Constitution of Éire is published. It allows for an elected Presidency and a two-house Parliament comprising a Legislature (the Dáil) and a vocationally based Senate.

A referendum accepts the New Constitution. Fianna Fáil comfortably win the General Election which is held at the same time as the referendum. The Constitution comes into effect on 29 December.

Irish volunteers in Spain fight on both sides in the month-long Battle of Jarama.

Foynes, on the Shannon estuary, is inaugurated as a flying boat stop on the transatlantic route.

The All Ireland Champions are Tipperary (hurling) and Kerry (football).

1938

Douglas Hyde becomes the first President of Ireland under the new Constitution.

There is a Free State General election after the Government
unexpectedly falls on the issue of civil service arbitration. Fianna
Fáil are returned with an increased majority.

The Trade War ends when the UK and Irish Governments negotiate
agreements on land loans, Treaty ports and economic issues. Ireland
regains possession of the British naval bases in Cork Harbour,
Berehaven and Lough Swilly.

Michael Donnellan founds the Clan na Talmhan Political Party.

Trolley-buses replace trams in Belfast.

Patrick Kavanagh publishes *The Green Fool*. Samuel Beckett
publishes *Murphy*.

The All Ireland Champions are Dublin (hurling) and Galway
(football).

1939

The IRA begin a bombing campaign in England (January). The
Coventry bomb kills five people (August).

The Irish Government outlaws the IRA. The Offences Against the
State Act establishes the Special Criminal Court for political
offenders.

World War II begins (1 September). The Dáil passes a Bill declaring
Ireland's neutrality on September 3, which sees the start of the
Emergency (the Second World War years in Ireland).

The UK Government decides not to extend conscription to Northern
Ireland after Catholic bishops state their opposition.

The Irish Red Cross is founded.

James Joyce publishes *Finnegan's Wake*. Flann O'Brien publishes *At
Swim Two Birds*.

The All Ireland Champions are Kilkenny (hurling) and Kerry
(football).

The death of William Butler Yeats (born 1865).

1940

John M. Andrews is appointed Northern Ireland Prime Minister.

The Irish Government introduces conscription.

Three people are killed in an accidental German bombing at Campile,
Co. Wexford.

German agent, Herman Goetz, is arrested and interned.

John Charles McQuaid becomes Catholic Archbishop of Dublin.

The All Ireland Champions are Limerick (hurling)and Kerry (football).
The deaths of James Craig (born 1871) and Roderick O'Connor (born
   1860), artist.

1941

Germans bombers target Belfast, killing almost 900 people (April/May).
   In the worst attack, 1,500 houses are destroyed and fire engines from
   Republican Ireland cross the border to help (15/16 April).
A German bomber mistakenly drops four bombs on Dublin – the largest
   lands on the North Strand and kills over 30 people (30/31 May).
The Terminal Building at Dublin Airport is completed (architect,
   Desmond Fitzgerald).
Kate O'Brien publishes *The Land of Spices.*
The All Ireland Champions are Cork (hurling)and Kerry (football).
The deaths of James Joyce (born 1882), Michael Healy (born 1873)
   and John Lavery (born 1856), artist.

1942

United States troops arrive in Northern Ireland. De Valera protests at
   their presence.
The Federated Union of Employers is founded in Dublin.
The Limerick Corporation begins demolishing parts of the Limerick
   'Lanes'.
The Irish Blood Transfusion Service is founded.
The statue 'The Virgin of the Twilight', now in Fitzgerald Park in
   Cork, is sculpted by Seamus Murphy.
Patrick Kavanagh publishes *The Great Hunger.* Eric Cross publishes
   The Tailor and Ansty.
The All Ireland Champions are Cork (hurling) and Dublin (football).

1943

In the General Election in Éire, Fianna Fáil is re-elected but does not
   have a clear majority.
Sir Basil Brooke is elected Prime Minister of Northern Ireland.
The Central Bank opens in Dublin.
A sea-plane en route to Foynes crashes on Mount Brandon, Co. Kerry,
   killing nine people.
The Northern Ireland Arts Council is set up.
The All Ireland Champions are Cork (hurling) and Roscommon
   (football).

1944

Fianna Fáil achieves a clear majority of 14 seats in the General
Election in Éire.

The National Labour Party is formed by breakaway Labour Party
members.

In the 'American Note' incident, the Irish Government refuses Allied
demands to expel German and Japanese diplomats.

The Children's Allowance is introduced for families with three or
more children.

Joyce Cary publishes *The Horse's Mouth*.

The All Ireland Champions are Cork (hurling) and Roscommon
(football).

The deaths of Joseph Campbell (born 1879), poet, and Eoin O'Duffy
(born 1892).

1945

Seán T. O'Kelly is elected President of Éire.

The end of World War II. It is estimated that almost 200,000 Irish-
born people served in the Allied Armed Forces.

Winston Churchill attacks Irish neutrality in World War II. De Valera
replies defending his position (May).

Córas Iompair Éireann (CIE), the national transport service, begins
operating.

The first transatlantic passenger flight arrives in Shannon Airport. Aer
Lingus transport 5,000 passengers during the year.

Kate O'Brien publishes *That Lady*.

The National Stud is established in Co. Kildare.

The All Ireland Champions are Tipperary (hurling) and Cork
(football).

The deaths of Count John McCormack (born 1884), Irish tenor, and
Eoin MacNéill (born 1867).

1946

Éirecensus: 2,955,000.

The Russians veto Ireland's application to join the United Nations.

Seán MacBride founds the Clann na Poblachta Party.

The Irish Government inaugurates the Departments of Health and
Social Welfare.

The Bord na Mona is established to exploit Ireland's peat resources.

The ESB begins the Rural Electrification Scheme.

Pan-American Airlines, BOAC and TWA begin regular flights into Shannon Airport.

The All Ireland Champions are Cork (hurling)and Kerry (football).

1947

The Republic of Ireland Health Act improves medical services and moots the controversial Mother and Child Scheme.

Shannon Airport is declared a Duty Free area.

Eamon Andrews begins his broadcasting career with Radio Éireann.

The All Ireland Champions are Kilkenny (hurling) and Cavan (football).

The death of James Larkin (born 1876).

1948

As a result of the General Election in Éire, Fine Gael and the Labour Party form an Administration under John A. Costello (the first Coalition Government in Ireland). Costello announces Ireland will become a Republic (September). The Republic of Ireland Act is passed (21 December).

An Taisce (the heritage and planning body) is established.

The Heat of the Day by Elizabeth Bowen is published.

The All Ireland Champions are Waterford (hurling)and Cavan (football).

1949

Éire officially becomes a Republic and leaves the Commonwealth.

The Ireland Act is passed in Britain, giving Irish citizens special status and confirming Northern Ireland will remain part of UK.

The Irish Government declines to compromise its neutrality by joining NATO.

The last Dublin to Dalkey tram runs.

The All Ireland Champions are Meath (hurling) and Tipperary (football).

The deaths of Douglas Hyde (born 1860) and Edith Somerville (born 1858), writer.

1950

Noel Browne proposes the Mother and Child Scheme. Catholic Bishops voice their disquiet in a letter to the Taoiseach.

The Irish and Northern Irish Governments co-operate to establish the Erne Drainage and Electrification Scheme.

The Irish DevelopmentAuthority (IDA) is founded to promote industrial growth.

The first turf-run power station opens in Portarlington.

In the Tilson Case, the Irish Supreme Court upholds the Catholic position on mixed marriage by ruling that parents have equal rights in deciding their child's religion, and prenuptial agreements have legal force.

The All Ireland Champions are Tipperary (hurling) and Mayo (football).

The deaths of James Stephens (born 1882), writer, and George Bernard Shaw (born 1856), who leaves a large sum to the National Gallery of Ireland.

1951

Census figures show that Republic of Ireland population stands at 2,961,000.

Roman Catholic bishops condemn the Mother and Child Scheme. It is abandoned and Noel Browne resigns.

After the General Eection in the Republic of Ireland, Fianna Fáil forms a new Government under De Valera.

Córas Tráchtála (the Irish Export Board) is established.

The Republic of Ireland Arts Council is set up.

The Abbey Theatre, Dublin, is destroyed by fire.

The Rev Ian Paisley forms the Free Presbyterian Church.

Professor E. Walton of Trinity College, Dublin, shares the Nobel Prize for Physics.

The All Ireland Champions are Tipperary (hurling) and Mayo (football).

1952

Seán T. O'Kelly begins his second term as President.

Legal adoption is introduced in the Republic of Ireland – the laws include clauses that prevent couples adopting children of a different religion and forbid couples in mixed marriages to adopt at all.

The Bord Faílte is established to encourage tourism in the Republic of Ireland.

The Irish Management Institution is founded in Dublin.

John Ford films *The Quiet Man* in Mayo.

The All Ireland Champions are Cork (hurling) and Cavan (football).

1953

Liam Kelly founds Fianna Uladh.

The *Princess Victoria* ferry disaster claims 128 lives on the Stranraer–
Larne route (January).

Radio Éireann inaugurates the annual Thomas Davis lectures on Irish
history and culture.

Gael-Linn is established to help revive spoken Irish.

The Irish Government bans newsreel films of the Coronation of Queen
Elizabeth II.

The Chester Beatty Library opens in Ballsbridge, Dublin, comprising
a collection of oriental and early manuscripts.

The Busárus Building, Dublin, is completed (architect, Michael Scott).

Samuel Beckett stages *Waiting for Godot*.

The All Ireland Champions are Cork (hurling) and Kerry
(football).

The death of Maud Gonne MacBride (born 1865).

1954

In the General Election in the Republic of Ireland, the Fine Gael and
Labour Coalition led by John T. Cosgrave ousts De Valera and
Fianna Fáil.

The flying of the Irish tricolour is effectively banned by the Northern
Ireland Parliament.

Liam Lynch founds Saor Uladh in Co. Tyrone.

Michael Manning becomes the last man to be hanged in the Republic
of Ireland.

The first appearance of myxamatosis – over the next decade, it almost
wipes out Ireland's rabbit population.

The National Stud buys the horse, Tulyar, for 200,000 pounds – a
world record at the time.

Brendan Behan stages *The Quare Fellow*.

Christie Brown publishes *My Left Foot*.

The All Ireland Champions are Cork (hurling) and Meath
(football).

1955

Ireland joins the United Nations.

Fire destroys Cork Opera House.

The first motorcars arrive on the Aran Islands.

Brian Moore publishes *The Lonely Passion of Judith Hearne*.

Christy O'Connor makes the first of ten successive appearances in the Ryder Cup golf competition (last appearance 1973).

The All Ireland Champions are Wexford (hurling) and Kerry (football).

The death of Evie Hone (born 1894), artist.

1956

Census in Republic of Ireland: 2,818,000.

The Republic of Ireland gives persons born in Northern Ireland after 1922 citizenship rights.

The IRA begins a new campaign of attacks in Northern Ireland.

The first of the annual Cork Film Festivals is held.

Ronnie Delaney wins a gold medal in the 1,500 metres at the Melbourne Olympics.

The All Ireland Champions are Wexford (hurling) and Galway (football).

1957

De Valera and Fianna Fáil are returned to power In the General Election in the Republic of Ireland.

Gaeltarra Éireann is founded to encourage the commercial and industrial growth of designated Gaeltacht (Irish speaking) areas.

At the first Dublin Theatre Festival, the staging of Tennessee Williams' *The Rose Tattoo* causes controversy.

The All Ireland Champions are Kilkenny (hurling) and Louth (football).

The deaths of Oliver St John Gogarty (born 1878), writer, and Jack B. Yeats (born 1871), artist.

1958

The first Irish Army soldiers serve in a United Nations peace-keeping mission (observers in the Lebanon).

The Industrial Development Act encourages foreign investment in the Republic of Ireland. Restrictions on outside ownership of industrial concerns are lifted.

Aer Lingus begins passenger services to United States (April).

The Ardmore Film Studio opens near Bray, Co. Wicklow.

The All Ireland Champions are Tipperary (hurling) and Dublin (football).

The deaths of Paul Henry (born 1876), artist, and Lennox Robinson (born 1886), dramatist.

1959

Eamon de Valera is elected the third President of the Republic of Ireland. Seán Lemass, Minister of Industry and Commerce, is appointed Taoiseach.

The CIU and ITUC union confederations reunify into the Irish Congress of Trade Unions.

The British and Irish Governments reach a compromise on the disputed pictures in the Hugh Lane Collection.

Seán Ríada composes the score for the film *Mise Éire*.

John B. Keane stages *Sive*.

The All Ireland Champions are Waterford (hurling) and Kerry (football).

1960

F. H. Boland assumes the Presidency of the General Assembly of the United Nations.

The 33rd battalion of the Irish Army joins the United Nations Peacekeeping Force in the Congo during the Congo Civil War.

In an ambush at Niemba, Baluba tribesmen attack an Irish patrol, killing nine Irish soldiers – only two survive (8 November).

Panama begin the first scheduled jetliner passenger service between the USA and Ireland.

Aer Lingus introduces the St Patrick, its first Boeing 707 jet, into service.

The All Ireland Champions are Wexford (hurling) and Down (football).

1961

The Irish Republic Census: 2,818,000. Northern Ireland Census: 1,426,000.

After the General Election in the Republic of Ireland, Seán Lemass forms a minority Fianna Fáil Government with the support of independent members.

Ireland joins UNESCO.

The Bord Bainne is set up to encourage milk production and marketing.

A State-owned television service is inaugurated by Radio Telefís Éireann (May).

The last of the Guinness Liffey steamers is taken out of service.

The West Clare Railway – the subject of Percy French's song 'Are Ye Right there Michael?' – closes down.

The All Ireland Champions are Tipperary (hurling) and Down
(football).

1962

The IRA abandons its six-year long campaign of attacks in Northern
Ireland.

Work begins on Liberty Hall, Dublin's first skyscraper (architect,
Desmond R. O'Kelly).

The first of Gay Byrne's weekly 'Late Late Shows' is broadcast by
RTE Television (6 July).

The All Ireland Champions are Tipperary (hurling) and Kerry (football).

1963

US President John F. Kennedy visits Ireland (June).

Terence O'Neill succeeds Lord Brookborough as Northern Ireland's
Prime Minister and leader of the Unionist Party.

William Conway is appointed Catholic Archbishop of Armagh.

11 June is the wettest day on record to date – 7.25 inches (186 mm) of
rain fall at Mount Merrion, Dublin.

Kilkenny Design Studios is set up.

Paddy Moloney forms the Chieftains – a traditional music group.

Shay Elliot becomes the first Irishman to wear the leader's yellow
jersey in the Tour de France.

The All Ireland Champions are Kilkenny (hurling) and Dublin
(football).

1964

The Second Programme for Economic Expansion is published in the
Republic of Ireland.

An Irish Army detachment is sent to the UN Peacekeeping Force in
Cyprus.

The Campaign for Social Justice is established in Northern Ireland.

The new American Embassy in Dublin is completed (architect, J. M.
Johansen).

The Ulster Folk Museum opens at Cultra, Co.Down.

Brian Friel stages *Philadelphia Here I Come*.

The All Ireland Champions are Tipperary (hurling) and Galway
(football).

The deaths of Maurice Walsh (born 1879), Brendan Behan (born
1923) and Seán O'Casey (born 1880).

1965

In the Republic of Ireland General Election, Fianna Fáil form the
Government with independent support.

Northern Ireland Prime Minister, Terence O'Neill, meets Irish
Taoiseach, Seán Lemass, in Dublin.

The human remains of Roger Casement are returned from England for
burial at Glasnevin.

The Clann na Poblachta Republican Party dissolves itself.

England and Ireland sign the Free-Trade Area Agreement.

The Nationalist Party in Northern Ireland enter Stormont as the
official opposition.

The Northern Ireland Government decides to build the new town of
Craigavon.

Aer Lingus fly 1,100,000 passengers this year, 200 times as many as
flew in 1945.

John B. Keane stages *The Field*.

The All Ireland Champions are Tipperary (hurling) and Galway (football).

The death of W. T. Cosgrave (born 1880).

1966

Jack Lynch succeeds Seán Lemass as Taoiseach.

Eamon de Valera is re-elected President.

Nelson's Pillar on O'Connell Street is blown up by Republicans –
pranksters steal Nelson's head.

Ulster Volunteer Force is founded in Northern Ireland.

Several banking groups merge to form the Allied Irish Bank.

The new Abbey Theatre is opened in Dublin.

Seamus Heaney publishes *Death of a Naturalist*.

In horse racing, Vincent O'Brien is the top flat trainer in Britain and
Arkle wins his third consecutive Cheltenham Gold Cup.

The All Ireland Champions are Cork (hurling) and Galway (football).

The deaths of Frank O'Connor (born 1903) and Flann O'Brien (real
name Brian Nolan, born 1911).

1967

The Northern Irish Civil Rights Association founded.

An Aer Lingus passenger plane crashes a few miles north of Dublin
Airport with three deaths.

Censorship is lifted on all books which have been banned for 12 years
or more.

The New Library at Trinity College, Dublin opens.

The first ROSC exhibition of contemporary art is held at the RDS, Dublin.

The Dubliners ballad group achieve international success after recording *Seven Drunken Nights*.

The All Ireland Champions are Kilkenny (hurling) and Meath (football).

The death of Patrick Kavanagh, poet (born 1904).

1968

Austin Curry occupies a council house in Caledon, Tyrone, to protest against the unequal allocation of Local Government housing.

The first major Civil Rights March takes place from Coalisland to Dungannon (24 August).

The People's Democracy is founded by student demonstrators at Queen's University, Belfast.

There is rioting in Derry (October).

The Northern Irish Government announces concessions to Catholics.

Terence O'Neill's moderate 'Ulster at the Crossroads' TV speech offends many Unionists and William Craig, Stormont Minister for Home Affairs, is dismissed.

The Tuskar Rock plane crash – 61 people are killed when the Aer Lingus plane *St Phelim* crashes into the Irish Sea.

The New University of Ulster opens in Coleraine.

Ireland's first planetarium opens at the Armagh Observatory.

Van Morrison releases *Astral Weeks*.

The All Ireland Champions are Wexford (hurling) and Down (football).

The deaths of W. J. Leech (born 1881), artist, and William O'Brien (born 1881), trade unionist.

1969

Fianna Fáil retain power in the General Election in the Republic of Ireland.

The Belfast to Derry Civil Rights March is ambushed at Burntollet Bridge (January 4).

There are riots in Derry (April, July). The first death occurs in the disturbances at Dungiven (14 July). British troops move into Derry after sectarian attacks on the Bogside (14/15 August). Last elections are held for the Northern Ireland Parliament. Terence O'Neill resigns as Unionist leader and is replaced by Major James Chichester-Clarke.

Protestant mobs and the B Specials attack Catholic areas in Belfast –
British Forces intervene to protect Catholic communities (15
August). The Belfast 'peace line' is established by the British Army.
The Hunt Report recommends the abolition of the B Specials and the
disarming of the RUC. The Ulster Defence Force is founded by militant
Loyalists. The UK Government issues the Downing Street Declaration.

Bernadette Devlin of the Unity Party, becomes the youngest MP to sit
in the British House of Commons.

The Republic of Ireland introduces special tax concessions for
creative artists and writers.

The Irish farthing and halfpenny coins cease to be legal tender.

The Wood Quay excavation of Viking Dublin begins.

Samuel Beckett wins the Nobel Prize for Literature.

The Clancy Brothers and the Tommy Makem ballad group disband.

John B. Keane stages *Big Maggie*.

James Plunkett publishes *Strumpet City*.

The All Ireland Champions are Kilkenny (hurling) and Kerry (football).

1970

Ministers Charles Haughey and Neil Blaney are dismissed from Jack
Lynch's Government for an alleged arms smuggling conspiracy
(neither minister is convicted in a later trial).

US President Richard Nixon visits Ireland. Gerry Fitt forms the Social
Democratic Labour Party in Northern Ireland.

The Republican Movement splits into the Provisional IRA and the
Official IRA.

The Ulster Defence Regiment replaces the B Specials.

Moderate Protestant and Catholics form the Alliance Party.

The Roman Catholic hierarchy removes its ban on Catholics attending
Trinity College, Dublin.

Irish banks go on strike for six months – many small businesses go
broke as a result.

'All Kinds of Everything', sung by Dana, wins Ireland the Eurovision
Song Contest

Van Morrison releases *Moondance*.

Christy O'Connor is selected as Texaco Golf Sportstar of the Year
(one of five times) and Supreme Sports Star. Nijinsky, trained by
Vincent O'Brien, become the first horse to win the English Classic
'grand slam' since 1935.

The All Ireland Champions are Cork (hurling) and Kerry (football).

1971
The first British soldier is killed in the current troubles (February 6).

Internment is introduced in Northern Ireland (9 August). By the end of
   year, 1,500 people have been placed in custody.

Brian Faulkner becomes Prime Minister of Northern Ireland. The Rev
   Ian Paisley forms the Democratic Unionist Party.

The Republic of Ireland adopts decimal coinage.

The 'Children of Lír' group (sculptor, Oísin Kelly) is unveiled in the
   Garden of Remembrance, Dublin.

Donal Lunney, Christie Moore, Liam O'Flynn and Andy Irvine form
   the seminal Irish folk group Planxty.

Mary Lavin publishes *Collected Stories*.

The All Ireland Champions are Tipperary (hurling) and Offaly (football).

The death of Seán Lemass (born 1899).

1972
Republic of Ireland voters opt to join the European Economic
   Community.

The voting age in the Republic is lowered from 21 to 18.

The Special Criminal Court (three judges, no jury) is initiated in
   Dublin to try political offences.

'Bloody Sunday' in Derry – 13 demonstrators are killed by soldiers of
   the Parachute Regiment (30 January).

The British Embassy in Dublin is burnt down during riots (2
   February).

The Northern Ireland Parliament is suspended in favour of direct rule
   by the British Parliament. William Whitelaw becomes first Secretary
   of State for Northern Ireland.

The 'Bloody Friday' bombings take place in Belfast – 19 people are
   killed and 130 injured (21 July). By the end of the year, the 'troubles'
   have claimed 678 lives since 1969.

A referendum removes the special status of the Catholic Church from
   the Irish Constitution.

The Irish Government introduces Value Added Tax.

The Irish Farmers Association is founded.

The NIHE, Limerick (now the University of Limerick), is officially
   opened.

Radio na Gaeltachta begins broadcasting.

Phil Lynott and Thin Lizzy have a UK hit with 'Whiskey in the Jar'.

Seamus Heaney publishes *Wintering Out*.

The All Ireland Champions are Kilkenny (hurling) and Offaly (football).

The death of Padraic Colum (born 1881), writer.

1973

The Republic of Ireland joins the EEC. Northern Ireland joins the
EEC with the United Kingdom.

As a result of the Republic of Ireland's General Election, a Fine Gael
and Labour Coalition is formed under Liam Cosgrave.

Erskine Childers becomes President of Ireland.

The *Claudia* arms shipment is intercepted by the Irish Navy.

Elections are held for the new Northern Ireland Power-sharing
Assembly. The Ulster United Unionist Council (UUUC) is founded
by the Orange Order, DUP and other Loyalist groups.

At the Sunningdale Conference, Northern Irish political parties, the
UK and the Republic of Ireland agree to establish a 'Council of
Ireland'.

The Irish Civil Service removes its bar on female employees
marrying.

The Supreme Court rules that the ban on importing contraceptives is
unconstitutional.

The compulsory pass in Irish is removed from the Intermediate and
Leaving Certificate Examinations.

Hugh Leonard stages *Da*.

The All Ireland Champions are Limerick (hurling) and Cork (football).

1974

Cearbhall O'Dalaigh becomes the fifth President of Ireland (unopposed).

Loyalist terrorists explode three bombs in the centre of Dublin (24
killed) and a fourth in Monaghan town (6 killed).

Ireland's biggest robbery to date takes place near Tralee, Co. Kerry –
75,000 pounds are stolen from a Post Office van.

The UUUC win 11 out of 12 Northern Irish seats in the British
General Election.

A Loyalist general strike closes electrical services and blockades
Belfast (May).

The Power-sharing Assembly is abandoned and the British
Government resumes direct rule.

An IRA attempt to tunnel out of the Maze Prison is foiled.

The Irish National Liberation Army is formed from militant dissidents in the Official IRA.

In the UK, the Guilford bombing leaves 5 dead and the Birmingham pub bombings 21 dead.

The new Central Bank building in Dublin is ordered to be lowered by 13 feet (4 metres) after planners find it has exceeded its permitted height.

An oil spillage from the tanker *Universal 1* threatens the West Cork coast.

Powerscourt House, Co. Wicklow, is burnt down.

Seán MacBride wins the Nobel Peace Prize.

The All Ireland Champions are Kilkenny (hurling) and Dublin (football).

The deaths of Kate O'Brien (born 1894) and Seamus Murphy (born 1907), sculptor.

1975

The IRA agree to a cease-fire in February, but it ends in November.

Elections are held for the Northern Ireland Constitutional Convention. The proposed assembly fails when the UUUC reject power sharing.

In the Miami Showband massacre, three band members and two UVF men are killed.

Internment in Northern Ireland ends (5 December).

The Herrema kidnapping and the Monasterevan siege take place (September–October).

Five people are killed in the Clogh Bridge train disaster in Co. Wexford.

The Blessed Oliver Plunkett, executed in 1681, is canonised.

The Druid Theatre, in Galway, opens.

The All Ireland Champions are Kilkenny (hurling) and Kerry (football).

The death of Eamon de Valera (born 1882).

1976

President O' Dalaigh resigns on a point of constitutional principle – he is replaced by Dr Patrick Hillery.

A report states that the Irish inflation rate is the highest in the EEC.

150,000 pounds are stolen in the Sallins mail train robbery.

Christopher Ewart-Biggs, the British Ambassador, and his secretary are killed by a landmine near his Rathfarnham residence.

In the Kingsmill massacre, Co. Armagh, ten Protestants are murdered in
  retaliation for the murder of five Catholics on the previous day.
The Peace People Movement is inaugurated in Belfast after three
  children die in a terrorist incident.
The 'blanket protest' is initiated by H Block Republican prisoners
  against the removal of their 'special category' political status.
A new Adoption Act permits couples in the Irish Republic to adopt
  children of a different religion.
Máiréad Corrigan and Betty Wilson, founders of the Peace People,
  win the Nobel Peace Prize.
Seamus Heany publishes *North*.
The All Ireland Champions are Cork (hurling) and Dublin (football).

1977

Fianna Fáil are re-elected with a clear majority in the General Election
  in the Republic of Ireland. Jack Lynch forms the Government. Dr
  Garret Fitzgerald succeeds Liam Cosgrave as leader of Fine Gael.
The Workers' Party is founded after a split in Sinn Fein.
1,400 jobs are lost in Limerick when the Ferenka factory closes down
  after a long-running industrial dispute.
The Treasures of Ireland Exhibition opens in the US.
Alex Higgins wins the World Professional Snooker Championship.
The All Ireland Champions are Cork (hurling) and Dublin (football).
The death of Seán Keating (born 1889), artist.

1978

An Irish Army battalion is sent to join the UN Peacekeeping Force in
  southern Lebanon.
Jack Lynch addresses the UN General Assembly.
David Cook of the Alliance Party is elected as Belfast's first non-
  Unionist Mayor.
In the La Mon hotel bombing in Co. Down, 16 people are killed.
The Matt Talbot Memoral Bridge opens in Dublin (the first new
  bridge to cross the Liffey since 1880).
The Dublin Institute of Technology (DIT) is founded. RTE 2, Ireland's
  second TV station, begins broadcasting.
Bob Quinn screens *Poitin* (an Irish language film).
Thin Lizzy release *Live and Dangerous*.
The All Ireland Champions are Cork (hurling) and Kerry (football).
The death of Mícheál Mac Liammóir (born 1899).

1979

The Republic of Ireland census: 3,365,000, an increase of 13%.

Jack Lynch retires from politics. He is replaced as leader of Fianna
  Fáil and Taoiseach by Charles Haughey (December).

European Parliament elections are held for the first time (15 seats in
  the Republic of Ireland). Sucessful candidates in Northern Ireland (3
  seats) include John Hume and the Rev Ian Paisley.

The French oil tanker *Betelgeuse* explodes at Whiddy Island Oil
  Refinery in Bantry Bay, killing 50.

The death of Lord Mountbatten and three others in the Mullaghmore
  boat bombing. On the same day, 18 British soldiers are killed in a
  bomb and gun attack at Warrenpoint, Co. Down (27 August).

The Irish Republic joins the European Monetary System which means
  the end of parity between sterling and the punt.

The Irish postal workers' strike lasts four months.

Pope John Paul II visits Ireland – 1,000,000 people attend an outside
  mass at Phoenix Park. In Drogheda, the Pope appeals for peace in
  Northern Ireland.

Tomás O' Fiaich, Archbishop of Armagh is appointed Cardinal.

The Irish Film Board is established.

Seamus Heaney publishes *Fieldwork*.

The All Ireland Champions are Kilkenny (hurling) and Kerry
  (football).

1980

Charles Haughey and British Prime Minister, Margaret Thatcher, establish
  the Anglo-Irish Committee at a summit meeting at Dublin Castle.

Nearly 700,000 Irish PAYE workers join in a day of protest at the
  unfair tax system.

A hunger strike is initiated by Republican prisoners in Northern
  Ireland. Cardinal O' Fiaich intervenes to avert deaths.

The Derrynafflan Chalice is discovered on a national monument site
  in Tipperary.

The Sense of Ireland Exhibition is held in London.

Brian Friel stages *Translations*.

The All Ireland Champions are Galway (hurling) and Kerry
  (football).

1981

The Republic of Ireland census: 3,443,405.

After the General Election in the Republic of Ireland, the Fine Gael and Labour Coalition form the Government under the leadership of Garret Fitzgerald. Margaret Thatcher and Garret Fitzgerald set up the Inter-governmental Council.

In the Stardust Ballroom disaster, 48 young people are killed in a fire at a Valentine's Night dance in Artane, Dublin.

The IRA Hunger Strike at the Maze Prison lasts from 9 March to 3 October. Deaths begin after 66 days. The following strikers die: Bobby Sands, the elected MP for South Fermanagh whilst on strike (5 May); Francis Hughes (12 May); Patsy O'Hara (21 May); Raymond McCreesh (21 May); Joseph McDonnell (8 June); Martin Hurson (13 July); Kevin Lynch (1 August); Kieran Doherty, elected TD for Cavan-Monaghan whilst on strike (3 August); Thomas McElwee (8 August); Michael Devine (20 August).

The National Concert Hall opens in Dublin.

Pat O'Connor makes the TV drama *Ballroom of Romance*.

The All Ireland Champions are Offaly (hurling) and Kerry (football).

The death of Christy Brown, writer.

1982

As a result of the February General Election in the Republic of Ireland, Charles Haughey forms a new Fianna Fáil Government but in the General Election in November, Garret Fitzgerald's Fine Gael and Labour Coalition are returned to power. Michael O'Leary resigns the leadership of the Labour Party and joins Fine Gael – he is replaced by Dick Spring.

Ireland refuses to participate in EEC trade sanctions on Argentina during the Falklands War.

Three IRA men are ambushed and killed by the RUC near Lurgan, Armagh and this incident is later alleged to be part of a 'shoot to kill' policy.

Droppin' Well pub bombing – INLA kill 11 off-duty soldiers and 6 civilians.

Corporal punishment is banned in Republic of Ireland schools.

Ireland win the Rugby Union Triple Crown Championship.

Alex Higgins wins the World Professional Snooker Tournament.

The All Ireland Champions are Kilkenny (hurling) and Offaly (football)

1983

The 'Bugging Scandal' – it is revealed that the previous Fianna Fáil administration placed wire taps on journalists Bruce Arnold and Geraldine Kennedy.

Inaugural meeting of the New Ireland Forum at Dublin Castle.

The Irish Republic appoints its first Ombudsman.

A policeman and a soldier are killed during the rescue of kidnap victim Don Tidey, following the most intensive manhunt in the history of the Irish Republic.

The race horse, Shergar, is kidnapped from Ballymany Stud, Newbridge, Kildare – he is never found.

The 'Supergrass' trials begin in Northern Ireland – 14 UVF members are convicted in the Joseph Bennet trial, and 22 IRA members in the Christopher Black trial.

Nine prisoners escape in a mass break-out from the Maze Prison – a warder is killed.

Two CIE trains crash outside of the town of Kildare and eight persons are killed.

The Irish Punt is devalued by 5%.

The Naas By-pass, the Irish Republic's first motorway, is opened.

A referendum is held on whether to place an anti-abortion amendment in the Irish Constitution – it is carried by 841,000 votes to 416,000.

The concept of illegitimacy is abolished in the Irish legal code.

Eamon Coughlan wins the 5,000 metres race at the Helsinki World Championships.

The All Ireland Champions are Kilkenny (hurling) and Dublin (football).

1984

US President Ronald Reagan visits Ireland.

The New Ireland Forum publishes a report suggesting three possible solutions for breaking the Northern Ireland impasse (May).

Dominick McGlinchey, accused of murdering three worshippers in Darkley Pentecostal Hall in 1983, is extradited from the Republic to Northern Ireland.

John Stalker begins an enquiry into the RUC killings of suspected Republican terrorists in Northern Ireland.

The IRA bomb the Conservative Party Conference at the Grand Hotel, Brighton (October).

Margaret Thatcher rejects the proposals of the New Ireland Forum in her 'Out! Out! Out!' speech (19 November).

The Department of Post and Telegraph is divided into An Post (postal services) and Telecom Éireann (telecommunications).

The Irish Shipping Company is liquidated. This heralds the end of the Irish merchant marine.

The East Link toll bridge is opened in Dublin. The famous Liffey ferry ceases its operations.

Natural gas from the Kinsale field begins to be pumped into Dublin.

The restoration of Kilmainham Hospital, Dublin, the finest seventeenth century building in Ireland, is completed.

Neil Jordan screens *Company of Wolves*.

U2 release *The Unforgettable Fire*.

John Tracey wins a silver medal in the marathon at the Los Angeles Olympic Games.

The All Ireland Champions are Cork (hurling) and Kerry (football).

The death of Liam O'Flaherty (born 1894).

1985

The Anglo-Irish Agreement is signed between the UK and the Republic of Ireland at Hillsborough (15 November).

Breakaway Fianna Fáil TDs and their supporters form the Progressive Democrat Party under the leadership of Desmond O'Malley.

An Air India Boeing 747 crashes into the sea 80 miles off the Irish coast after a bomb explodes on board – all 329 people on board are killed.

The Insurance Corporation of Ireland is in crisis – the Irish Government intervenes with financial guarantees to protect the Allied Irish Bank.

Knock Regional Airport, Mayo, receives its first commercial flight (official opening 1986).

The phenomena of 'moving statues' arises – a shrine to the Virgin Mary at Ballinspittle, Co Cork, attracts thousands of pilgrims.

Dublin musician, Bob Geldof, organises the Live Aid Concert to raise funds for victims of the Ethiopian Famine.

Ireland defeat England in Dublin to win the Rugby Triple Crown.

Barry McGuigan defeats Eusebio Pedroza to become the WBA featherweight champion of the world.

The All Ireland Champions are Offaly (hurling) and Kerry (football).

1986

Republic of Ireland census: 3,541,000.

John Stalker is removed from his enquiry into the RUC killings – there are allegations of a 'cover-up' by the British Intelligence Services.

The Belfast Appeals Court overturns the convictions in the Christopher Black 'Supergrass' trial.

The national transport company, CIE, is restructured into separate Bus, Rail and Dublin Bus services.

A Goya and a Vermeer are amongst ten paintings stolen from the Beit Collection at Russborough House in a robbery masterminded by the Dublin criminal the 'General'.

The ore carrier *Kowloon Bridge* runs ashore on one of the most beautiful stretches of the Dingle Peninsula, Kerry.

Hurricane Charlie, the worst summer storm in living memory, causes unprecedented damage.

A referendum in the Republic of Ireland rejects a constitutional amendment to permit divorce.

The Pro-life Movement takes court action under the Constitutional Amendment to prevent Family Planning clinics advising on abortion facilities abroad.

Pine martens, thought to be extinct in Ireland, are discovered in the Killarney National Park.

The All Ireland Champions are Cork (hurling) and Kerry (football).

The death of Phil Lynott, rock musician.

1987

A General Election is held in the Republic of Ireland when the Labour Party withdraws from the coalition. A new Fianna Fáil Government is formed under Charles Haughey. Garret Fitzgerald resigns from leadership of Fine Gael and he is succeeded by Alan Dukes.

Irish Republic referendum approves the Single Eurpean Act.

The British army kills eight IRA members and a civilian in an ambush at Loughgall, Co. Armagh.

Enniskillen bombing – 11 people are killed whilst attending a Remembrance Day service at the War Memorial. The *Eksund*, smuggling 150 tons of arms from Libya to Ireland for the IRA, is arrested by French authorities. A nationwide search for other arms dumps follows.

Ireland's national debt spirals towards 260 billion pounds – Fianna
Fáil implement a policy of cutbacks in Government expenditure.

The Poulnabrone portal tomb is excavated in Co. Clare.

U2 release *The Joshua Tree*.

Stephen Roche becomes the first Irish cyclist to win the Tour de France.
He also wins the World Championship at Villich, Austria, this year.

Marcus O'Sullivan wins the first of three 1,500 metres at the World
Indoor Championships (others 1989, 1993).

The All Ireland Champions are Galway (hurling) and Meath (football).

The death of Eamon Andrews (born1922), boxer and broadcaster.

1988

John Hume, leader of the SDLP, holds a meeting with Gerry Adams of
Sinn Féin. He is criticised by other Northern Ireland political parties.

A Loyalist gunman kills three mourners at an IRA funeral in Milltown
Cemetery, Belfast. Two days later, two British soldiers are dragged
from their car and murdered by the IRA.

The Irish Government brings in a harsh budget to deal with the
worsening economic crisis. A tax amnesty in the Republic of Ireland
raises 500 million pounds.

Aer Ríanta, the State-owned airport maintenance company, negotiates
a contract to service the Aeroflot fleet at Shannon and to open duty
free shops in Moscow and Leningrad Airports.

The Grange Development wins compensation of two million pounds
from Dublin County Council when they are refused planning
permission on land they own.

Dublin celebrates its Millennium; the Anna Livia sculpture is unveiled
in O'Connell Street and soon gets the nickname 'the Floozie in the
Jacuzzi'.

The Republic of Ireland football team reach the European Cup Finals
in Germany. They beat England 1–0 but do not progress beyond the
first stage.

The All Ireland Champions are Galway (hurling) and Meath (football).

The death of Seán MacBride (born 1904).

1989

As a result of the General Election in The Republic of Ireland, Charles
Haughey forms a coalition Fianna Fáil and Progressive Democrat
Government.

Peter Brooke is appointed Secretary of State for Northern Ireland.

Mikhail Gorbachev, leader of the Soviet Union, makes a short visit to
Ireland when his plane is refuelling at Shannon Airport.

Johnston, Mooney and O'Brien, Dublin's oldest and best-known
bakery, closes down.

Century Radio, Ireland's first independent national radio station to
operate legally, begins broadcasting.

Jim Sheridan releases *My Left Foot*.

Marcus O'Sullivan establishes a new world record in the indoor 1,500
metres.

The All Ireland Champions are Tipperary (hurling) and Cork
(football).

The death of Samuel Beckett (born 1906).

1990

Mary Robinson is elected the Republic of Ireland's first female
President.

John Bruton replaces Alan Dukes as leader of Fine Gael.

Brian Keenan, held hostage in Beirut for several years, is released and
returns to Ireland.

The Republic of Ireland football team reach the World Cup Finals for
the first time – they lose 1–0 to Italy in the quarter-finals.

Alan Parker releases *The Commitments*.

Roddy Doyle publishes *The Snapper*.

Brian Friel stages *Dancing at Lughna*sa.

The deaths of Cardinal Tomás O' Fiaich and Terence O'Neill (born
1904).

1991

Republic of Ireland census: 3,526,000.

An investigation is launched into alleged fraud and malpractice in the
beef industry.

The Irish Government allows US airforce planes to refuel at Shannon
Airport during the Gulf War.

The 'Birmingham Six', wrongly accused of involvement in the 1974
pub bombings, are released from prison in England. The convictions
of the 'Maguire Seven' are quashed.

UVF gunmen murder three people at a mobile shop in Craigavon, Co.
Armagh.

The legal age for purchasing condoms is reduced to 17 – their sale is
permitted in pubs and discos.

Eddie Jordan sets up his Formula 1 racing team.

Sonia O'Sullivan establishes a new world record in the 5,000 metres.

The All Ireland Champions are Tipperary (hurling) and Down
(football).

1992

Charles Haughey resigns and is replaced as Taoiseach by Albert
Reynolds (February).

The Republic of Ireland General Election results in no clear majority
(November).

The Irish public overwhelmingly approve the Maastricht Treaty in a
referendum.

The Democratic Left Party is formed after the Workers' Party split
(Febuary).

The UDA are banned in Northern Ireland.

Nelson Mandela visits Ireland.

The X Case – the Supreme Court allows a 14 year-old-girl to travel to
England for an abortion. There are further referendums on the
abortion issue (3 held simultaneously).

Eamon Casey, Bishop of Galway, resigns after it is revealed that he is
the father of a teenage son.

Neil Jordan screens *The Crying Game*.

Barcelona Olympic Games – Michael Carruth wins a gold boxing
medal (welterweight) and Wayne McCullough wins a silver boxing
medal (bantamweight).

The All Ireland Champions are Kilkenny (hurling) and Donegal
(football).

1993

The Fianna Fáil and Labour Coalition forms a Government under
Albert Reynolds.

Mary Harney succeeds Desmond O'Malley as leader of the PD party.

The Downing Street Declaration is signed by Albert Reynolds and John
Major.

The Shankill Road bombing kills ten people in Belfast. Loyalist
gunmen shoot six Catholics in retaliation within a week. The UVF
kill six people when they open fire in the Rising Sun public house.

The Irish punt is devalued after it is targeted by currency speculators.

The budget deficiency in the Irish Republic has been reduced to 250 million pounds.

Homosexuality is decriminalised in the Republic of Ireland.

Jim Sheridan releases *In the Name of the Father*.

Roddy Doyle publishes *Paddy Clarke Ha Ha Ha* (it wins the Booker Prize in London).

The All Ireland Champions are Kilkenny (hurling) and Derry (football).

1994

A new Fine Gael and Labour Party Coalition Government is formed under John Bruton after the Labour Party withdraws its support from Fianna Fáil. Bertie Ahern replaces Albert Reynolds as leader of Fianna Fáil. The broadcasting ban on Sinn Féin is lifted by the Irish and UK Governments.

The IRA cease-fire is inaugurated (30 August). Loyalist cease-fire is inaugurated (October 13).

The Forum for Peace and Reconciliation meets in Dublin.

The Emegency Powers Act in the Republic is revoked.

The Irish Government releases nine IRA prisoners.

The RTE TV drama *The Family*, with a script by Roddy Doyle, is broadcast.

Frank Delaney publishes *The Sins of the Mothers*.

Catherine McKiernan wins the last of four consecutive victories in the annual World Cross Country Grand Prix Series. Sonia O'Sullivan establishes a new world record for the 2,000 metres.

Ireland reach the last 16 of the Football World Cup Finals in the USA before they are defeated by Holland.

The All Ireland Champions are Offaly (hurling) and Down (football).

1995

The Framework Document for Northern Ireland is launched by John Bruton and John Major.

US President Clinton visits Northern Ireland and Dublin to help support the peace process.

A referendum in the Republic of Ireland legalises divorce by the narrowest of margins – a majority of only 9,100 out of 1,630,000 votes cast.

The Irish Republic legalises the provision of information and advice on abortion.

Daytime British Army patrols end in Belfast.

The Irish Supreme Court allows the family of a woman who has been in a coma for 20 years to withdraw her life support system.

Steve Collins beats Chris Eubank to win the WBO Super Middleweight title.

The All Ireland Champions are Clare (hurling) and Dublin (football).

1996

Republic of Ireland census: 3,621,000.

Ireland assumes the Presidency of the European Union (July–December).

The Sunday Independent crime journalist, Veronica Guerin, is murdered by a drugs gang she has been investigating.

The IRA cease-fire ends with the Canary Wharf bombings in London.

Detective Sergeant Jerry McCabe is murdered by an armed gang in Adare, Co. Limerick (convictions secured 1999).

Elections to the Northern Ireland Forum are held. Stormont multi-party talks begin (June).

Orange marchers confront local Catholics at Drumcree, Co. Down, over the right to march down the Garvaghy Road (July).

Telifis na Gaeilge (the Irish language TV service) is launched.

Ireland wins the Eurovision Song Contest for the 4th time in five years.

Seamus Heaney wins the Nobel Prize for Literature.

Neil Jordan screens *Michael Collins*.

Frank McCourt publishes *Angela's Ashes*.

Michelle Smith wins three gold swimming medals at the Los Angeles Olympic Games.

The All Ireland Champions are Wexford (hurling) and Meath (football).

1997

Mary MacAleese is elected President – Ireland's second female president. As the result of the Republic of Ireland General Election, Bertie Ahern forms a Fianna Fáil and Progressive Democrat Coalition Government.

The McCracken Tribunal investigates payments to politicians.

Father Brendan Smith is gaoled for 12 years for sexual offences in the Republic of Ireland.

Constables John Grahame and David Andrew Johnston become the
   300th and 301st RUC men to be murdered in the current troubles.

Sinn Féin candidates win two seats in the UK House of Commons.

The IRA announces a new cease-fire.

The effects of the BSE cattle disease scare are estimated to have cost
   the economy of the Republic of Ireland up to 1 billion pounds.

The All Ireland Champions are Clare (hurling) and Kerry (football).

1998

The Good Friday Agreement is signed by all parties in Northern
   Ireland.

The first all-Ireland ballot since 1918 approves the Good Friday
   Agreement (94.39% in the Republic and 71.12% in the North).

A new enquiry into 'Bloody Sunday' is announced by the UK
   Government.

The three Quinn children die in a Loyalist arson attack in Ballymoney,
   Co. Antrim.

A car bomb planted by a dissident IRA group at Omagh, Co. Tyrone,
   kills 29 people.

SDLP leader John Hume and Ulster Unionist leader David Trimble
   jointly receive the Nobel Peace Prize.

The booming economy of the Republic of Ireland becomes known as
   the 'Celtic Tiger'.

The Irish Government implement measures to deal with huge
   increases in house prices.

The Freedom of Information Act is passed in the Republic of Ireland.

A monument to Ireland's First World War dead is opened in Belgium.

Pat O'Connor screens *Dancing at Lughnasa*.

The first stages of the Tour de France are held in Ireland.

The Irish under-16 and under-18 football teams win the European
   Championships.

The All Ireland Champions are Offaly (hurling) and Galway
   (football).

1999

Ireland adopts the euro as currency.

There are confrontations in Portadown following an official banning
   on the Orange Order parade at Drumcree.

The Irish economy's growth rate of 7% is the highest in Europe.

The Patten Report on the future of the Royal Ulster Constabulary
  makes many recommendations including name and badge change.
Jack Lynch, a former Taoiseach, dies.
It is announced that the RUC is to be awarded the George Cross.
Power is devolved to the elected Northern Ireland Assembly (2
  December).
The British-Irish Agreement creates a North–South Ministerial
  Council and other cross-border institutions.
The All Ireland Champions are Cork (hurling) and Meath (football).

2000
The deadlock over the decommissioning of terrorist weapons brings
  about the suspension of the Northern Ireland Assembly and the
  reimposition of direct rule (February).
Inflation in the Irish Republic runs at 5.5% (June).
Lawyers in Northern Ireland are no longer obliged to swear an oath to
  the Queen.
The Northern Ireland Assembly resumes its functions (June).
Eleven people die in road accidents during the Republic's August
  Bank Holiday.
Poor Irish results in the Sydney Olympic Games provoke a
  reassessment of the country's athletic training programme.
Newspaper headlines in the Republic throughout the year are
  dominated by reports on scandals in the worlds of politics and
  commerce. The Government commissions the Flood Report on
  ethics in public life.
Outgoing US President Bill Clinton makes his third visit to Dublin
  and Belfast.
The All Ireland Champions are Kilkenny (hurling) and Kerry
  (football).

Index

Index

B

M

N

P